D1642350

C152965872

LETTERS
FROM AN
EARLY BIRD

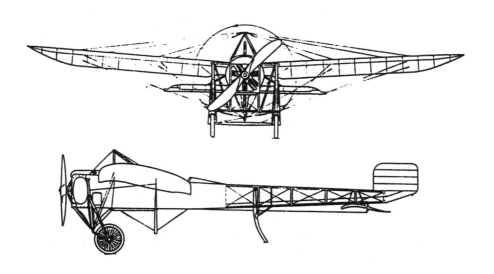

Blériot XI

LETTERS
FROM AN
EARLY BIRD

The life and letters of aviation pioneer
Denys Corbett Wilson 1882–1915

Donal MacCarron

Pen & Sword
AVIATION

First published in Great Britain in 2006 by
Pen & Sword Aviation
an imprint of
Pen & Sword Books Ltd

Copyright © Donal MacCarron, 2006

ISBN 1 84415 382 7
978 1 84415 382 4

British Library Cataloguing-in-Publication Data
A CIP catalogue record for this book is
available from the British Library

Typeset in Palatino by
Phoenix Typesetting, Auldgirth, Dumfriesshire

Printed and bound in England by
CPI UK

Pen & Sword Books   rd Aviation,
Pen & Sword Mar   al History,
Pen & Sword Se   Cooper.

For a cor   :t

47 Church S   gland

Contents

Acknowledgements   vii

Foreword Base   ix

Preface   xi

1   The Corbett Wilsons   1

2   Gaining his Wings   5

3   The Man and his Machine   9

4   The Challenge   13

5   The Crossing   17

6   Another Rival: Vivian Hewitt   21

7   In Irish Skies   23

8   CW Joins Up   27

9   European Adventures   31

10   The RFC Flies Off to War   35

11   Letters: 13 August to 4 November 1914   41

12   Forward Base   71

13   Letters: 5 to 24 November 1914   73

14   Lt-Col Robert Loraine, RFC   89

15   Letters: 25 November to 25 December 1914   91

16   Silent Night – Hilarious Day   113

17   Letters: 28 December 1914 to 26 January 1915   115

18   Moranes, at Last!   137

19   Letters: 6 to 17 February 1915   139

20   The First Battle   147

21   Letters: 26 April to 9 May 1915   153

22   The Last Battle   165

23   Envoi   167

24   Remembrance   171

       Index   173

Acknowledgements

At the top of this list must come Richard Corbett who lived at East Grinstead in Surrey some forty years ago. He was a first cousin of Denys Corbett Wilson and he generously placed the pioneer's letters and other ephemera at my disposal.

I also acknowledge Air Marshal Sir Freddie Sowrey, for his help and encouragement and for capturing the spirit of the work in his Foreword. Sir Freddie was for many years the President of Cross & Cockade International, the premier group of historians on the air war of 1914–18.

A special thanks to Paul Williams in Wales who made his photo collection available. Paul produced a commemorative booklet for the 75th anniversary of CW's crossing but did not include the letters. For his enhancement of illustrations I found an expert in Greg Stockdale. In Ireland, my thanks to Madeleine O'Rourke, aviatrix extraordinaire, and to P.J. Cummins.

Two stalwarts in the Archives of the RAF Museum at Hendon are Peter Elliott and Andrew Renwick whom I couple with Jack Long, the chronicler of No. 3 Squadron RFC/RAF, the premier British squadron, in thanking them for their support.

I send paternal greetings to my son John MacCarron, acknowledging his gentle prodding to get the book done, and for his computer expertise.

Finally, I claim for myself any acciderital omissions in the above list, and any errors elsewhere in the book.

DMacC
Gerrards Cross
February 2006

Foreword

Air Marshal Sir Frederick Sowrey KCB, CBE, AFC
(Past President of Cross & Cockade International)

Writing a foreword for an era out of one's time is never simple. Attitudes, social conventions and even words change and this is particularly so in flying. Here, personal experience is further up the scale of development of a phenomena which is barely one hundred years old. However in any period there is an immediate kinship with the persistent pioneers like Denys Corbett Wilson. He was also a trailblazer. His landmark crossing of the Irish Sea by air and work in introducing flying to Ireland are of historical importance at a time when every flight was a step forward in knowledge.

As an early member of the Royal Flying Corps in 1913 he helped to set the conditions for the expansion to 22,000 aircraft four years later. This growth was only possible for an organisation confident in its own ability to absorb the four generations of aircraft development compressed into the war years.

Descriptions of early flying can be technical but lack the human touch. However these 'Letters From an Early Bird' combine both, and add a fascinating relationship between mother and son which contains much of the minutiae of everyday life which is normally absent. What shines from the pages is enthusiasm and courage with the fearless ability to 'fly anything with wings on it'. Additionally, Corbett Wilson was a strategic thinker with a practical scheme to bomb Berlin – a formative use of air power.

Perhaps the greatest importance is to show the thoughts and feelings of one of the first men at war in a new environment and his relationship in this maelstrom with the woman who bore him. His tenderness for her safety and well-being; his love of animals; his concerns for his own men as well as a realistic approach to his enemies show an individual whose death after ten months of conflict robbed us all of a man who would have continued to chronicle the first war in the air with truth and sensitivity.

Preface

Some forty years ago as a writer with an interest in aviation, particularly anything pertaining to my native Ireland, I became aware of the exploits of Denys Corbett Wilson, a pioneer in the new art of powered flight. Luckily I met one of his nephews who provided me with copies of the letters which the pilot had sent to his widowed mother during the early days of the Great War. This collection forms the corpus of my book for which I take no credit. Thanks to DCW's keen observations, we are given a unique account of the first air war fought, on both sides, in aircraft which were not very far removed from that of the Wright Brothers a mere decade earlier. I have not attempted to edit the letters other than to include some explanatory notes. I have, however, prepared some chapters as background to the exciting life of an experienced aviation pioneer and his later wartime exploits.

Readers who travel in the comfort of today's aircraft, even in the sometimes cramped seats of economy class, cannot conceive of the spartan conditions endured in the exposed cockpit of a Bleriot. Perhaps this can be compared to cycling downhill at speed into a strong icy wind? There the comparison ends. Pedal power is unlikely to give out and at a few feet above terra firma is remote from an uncontrollable descent from on high caused by engine or structural failure or bad weather. And cycling is a peaceful pursuit, usually free from hostile firepower!

Of course, a pleasant flight on a bright summer day could

also be experienced with the added bonus of sailing over the picturesque landscape at unheard-of speeds. But the hazards faced by early aviators who sought to emulate the birds in the rudimentary flying machines of the early 1900's were enormous. A robust courage was required.

In CW's adopted country the new art of aviation was centred on Dublin where a notable air display took place in 1910, followed two years later by 'The Great Flying Race from Dublin to Belfast – and Back'. The catalogue for this event declared: 'The Aero Club of Ireland has characteristically seen to it that the profits (from the earlier event) should only be a means to a further end. The monies so made have served to keep together the band of pioneer enthusiasts and believers until they have grown in the brief space of two years to a well-established body . . . '.

Further south, CW was entertaining huge crowds with his flights – while keeping an eye on developments elsewhere. In August 1913 another pioneer, Harry Hawker had a 'walkover' in a somewhat abortive 'Round Britain Seaplane Race' which provoked an article by the editor of *The Irish Times* entitled 'The Strain of Flight'. CW's response to this ran as follows: 'In your leading article of your issue of 19th August, you enumerate various difficulties to be met with in such a contest, and go on to say that the chief of these is the continued strain, to the pilot, in a long flight. For human weakness there is no remedy – this, a propos of Mr. Hawker's four hours' flight, with one stop, from Southampton to Yarmouth in a Sopwith Seaplane. Now, I do not wish to belittle a fine performance, but in discussing "long flights" and the strain of such to the pilot, I should like to remind you of, and of necessity compare, flights put up by French aviators . . .'. CW went on to enumerate a long list of flights on the Continent which had lasted non-stop up to eight hours. He continued: 'When considering these flights, one must remember that they were over every imaginable kind of country, from the Ardennes to the Pyrenees . . . I write at length, as in my opinion nothing is gained by writing articles in which a four hours' flight, with a stop, is cited as an unheard of strain. Look at the map of Europe, and remember what our friends over the water are doing every day'.

Corbett Wilson was giving a wake-up call to Britain which he considered to be over complacent. He was imbued with the hopes and spirit of the true pioneer. A poet encapsulated this attitude in the following lines:

From Icarus to Bacon we dared the deadly quest,
With courage never shaken by failure manifest;
So strove to sail the glad air, so passed the torch alight
From Caley unto Ader, to Langley, Roe and Wright.

Donal MacCarron 2006

CHAPTER ONE

The Corbett Wilsons

This is the tale of an early pioneer aviator who took to the air just a few years after the Wright brothers proved that man was capable of controlled powered-flight. He was an Anglo-Irishman named Denys Corbett Wilson – the only child of a wealthy family. He was born on 24 September 1882 at Thames Ditton, Surrey, a prosperous town in the environs of London. His mother was Ada Caroline Wilson, née Corbett, from County Kilkenny. His father was William Henry Charles Wilson, a successful barrister known as 'Carlos'. The extended family enjoyed a life of Edwardian elegance.

Their Surrey home, Imber Court, had belonged to Carlos's grandfather since 1861 and remained so until the end of the century. Part of the estate is now the Headquarters of the London Metropolitan Mounted Police, but the house itself was demolished in the 1920s. The new baby was registered as 'Corbett Wilson' without a hyphen, though on the birth certificate his mother signed herself 'A.C. Wilson'. However, after the demise of Carlos, mother and son adopted the surname 'Corbett Wilson'.

The Corbett Wilsons were well connected and their extended family was prominent in public life. Like Carlos, an uncle of Denys was a barrister and Liberal MP for East Grinstead in Surrey from 1906 to 1910. Another uncle, though a barrister (the law seemed to run in the family), was primarily a novelist and naval historian who became Sir Julian Wilson. On the distaff side there was also a barrister: Margery Corbett who was created a Dame in 1967.

But now to the central character, Denys, who will be often referred to as 'CW' throughout this book. He was at Eton from 1896 to 1899; he did not distinguish himself there. He was later to show his sporting side, principally horse riding, boating, motoring and the new adventure of aviation. After Eton, he was commissioned into the Dorset Regiment – not one of the 'good' regiments like the Guards. He served with the Dorset's 3rd Battalion whose battles included the Relief of Ladysmith in the South African War. By the end of that conflict CW had transferred to the Royal Regiment of Artillery as a Lieutenant in 1908.

CW resigned his commission and he and his mother went to live at Lake Chrissie in the Transvaal. Eventually, they had had enough of sunny climes and returned to London life before they moved to his mother's native county, Kilkenny. They rented Darver House, Jenkinstown, not far from her birthplace. CW had another Irish connection: Charles Joseph Corbett of Imber Court, who in 1852 had married Elizabeth Byrne from Co. Wicklow.

Darver House became the centre of life for the wealthy landed gentry of the county. There was a sizeable staff, one of whom acted as chauffeur for their motor car, a high-powered Ralle, when CW himself was not driving it at high speeds. Motor cars were then very much a novelty and they brought out a love of technology that CW had always harboured. He also indulged in the usual pursuits of a country gentleman – huntin', shootin' and fishin'. A natural horseman, CW hunted with the Kilkenny pack and the Queen's County Hounds (Co. Offaly) and was a frequent race-goer. Out with the hounds, he was involved in at least two incidents: he was thrown off into a quarry and had to be carried home unconscious. On another occasion both he and his mount had to be extricated with ropes from a bog. Neither incident was the cause of a slight limp – a consequence of a minor wound received during the Boer War.

Despite his army service and the horrors he subsequently

witnessed during the Great War, CW remained a quiet, gentle, somewhat reticent man, possibly the result of being an only child. His letters to his mother, which form the *corpus* of this book, show his concern for his fellow man, particularly those serving in the dreadful conditions of the trenches. He loved animals and one is touched by his constant enquiries about his dog Jock, quarantined for several months after both he and his mother returned to England on the outbreak of war. This handsome man liked the ladies: in his letters, there are mentions of a Nicole who was the reason for a visit that led him on a flight over the Jura Alps – an aviation first. There was also an apparently lively lass to whom he gave the nickname 'Naughty'! However, his crowded life and eventual death over the Western Front precluded any marriage.

CHAPTER TWO

Gaining his Wings

When Louis Bleriot flew the English Channel from his native France to Britain in July 1909, his aeroplane was the basic Bleriot Mk XI. His record flight made him the world's leading aircraft manufacturer up until 1914. He quickly foresaw that the market for his machines would be limited unless he could also offer flying tuition as well as his machines. He was quick to organise two flying schools at two sites in France.

Bleriot's brochure stated:

We have now established in France two Schools of Piloting: one at Pau, the other at Etampes. Our school at Pau [near the Pyrenees] operates during the winter when the weather does not allow flying in the neighbourhood of Paris. We have chosen Pau because of its quite exceptional situation and because of its ideal winter temperatures. When the fine weather returns we bring our school back to Etampes, 60 kilometres from Paris, in the great plain of La Beauce, well-suited to enable young aviators to make fine flights, while running as few risks as possible. We have just opened at Hendon, near London, a third school for our customers in England.

This brochure also gave three pages of advice about learning to fly.

Corbett Wilson enrolled in the school at Pau, which by the spring of 1911 was a going concern with hangars and ancillary buildings. The 'winter' and 'summer' aerodromes were manned by the best personnel from Bleriot's aircraft manufacturing facility – which, of course, affected both the manufacturing and commercial sides of his enterprises. Bleriot believed in delegating, for instance handing over the complete management of both schools to an employee, Ferdinand Collin, who was basically a mechanic. Collin remembered his boss leaving him at one site saying:

> There you are, you are in charge of the school, of the hangars that are going to be built, of the aeroplanes, of the supplies, of the staff, and of the pupils I will send you. Au revoir, Ferdinand, sort things out for yourself and work hard!

Both schools provided a four-stage training programme. The first stage involved learning about the engine with the aircraft standing on the ground. The second stage involved taxiing in a straight line using the rudder only in a machine with rudimentary wings dubbed 'The Penguin' – this to prevent an accidental take-off! Next, the pupil had to take off and fly at a height between 1 and 6 metres, and land again – all more or less in a straight line. Finally, to get their wings, fledgling pilots had to satisfy the French Aero Club by flying three circles of 1 kilometre each, all on different days. Later, these circuits were increased to a radius of 5 kilometres, and landings had to be made within 150 metres of a point marked on the aerodrome.

A bright pupil with a spell of favourable weather could accomplish all this in eight days; but the less able, particularly if bedevilled by bad weather, could take up to six weeks. Total flying time was only from 2 to 5 hours, in lessons lasting between 10 and 15 minutes. Surprisingly, it was not the more difficult latter stages of training that caused the most trouble.

The Bleriot XI was not inclined to follow a straight path when taxiing or taking off because the undercarriage had castering wheels whose purpose was to facilitate landing in a side wind. Ground movements were also not helped, because at low speeds the rudder was almost impotent.

Tutored by *Monsieur* Henri Selmet, Corbett Wilson soon won his wings. He liked the Bleriot XI to the extent of buying one; the type had been greatly improved since the cross-channel record. Purchasers did not have to pay for training but would be responsible for the repair of any damage to the school machines. Louis Bleriot had a very tight contract stating this condition, while absolving his company from virtually everything else!

Aspiring aviators came to the schools from all over, and in CW's words 'Pau was an absolute Tower of Babel'. There were approximately seventy pupils there of whom about half obtained their brevets or 'wings' insignia. There were forty-two aeroplanes in the inventory, twenty-eight owned by pupils and fourteen by the school which was staffed by sixty personnel. Activity was intense and on one day CW counted a total of fifteen aeroplanes all in the air at one time. The two French schools remained in operation until 1920.

New and visionary technical ideas kept the Bleriot enterprise going: mechanical invention, Bleriot's passion in youth, continued to burn into his middle years. He died at the age of 64, having suffered a heart attack at his home on 1 August 1936.

CHAPTER THREE

The Man
and his Machine

The Bleriot XI purchased by CW was a frail-looking machine compared with other contemporary types. Nevertheless, it was a very advanced shoulder-wing monoplane design which, with increased power and slight modifications, became the most popular 'tractor' (propeller in the nose) aircraft of the pre-Great War days. It was relatively small with a length of 23 ft 6 in and a wingspan of 25 ft 7 in. The wings were a series of thin wooden members braced by wire and covered with fabric. The fuselage was a wire-braced box-girder of ash wood left uncovered at the front but fully enclosed from just behind the wings. The engine supports were formed by tubular metal framework, as was the undercarriage which mounted a pair of bicycle wheels. A small tail wheel was fitted.

The control system was rudimentary: lateral control was achieved by 'warping' the outer trailing edges of the wings, which would allow the aircraft to be banked – i.e. dipped from side-to-side. Lateral control by means of wing warping could only be a temporary expedient because the constant flexing of the tips of the wings would, sooner or later, weaken the structure until permanent distortion affected the aeroplane's performance. All constructors searched for something more workmanlike, and hinged 'ailerons' on the trailing edges eventually became the norm. The early version of the Mk. XI in which Bleriot accomplished the Channel crossing was powered (if that's the right word!) by an Ansani engine driving a 6 ft 6 in propeller, which could deliver 1400 revs. Total loaded weight was 660 lb and a speed of 36 mph could be achieved. The price for this early basic machine, *sans engine*, was £480 and its cross-channel success ensured that many customers were willing to pay this amount.

The first international aviation meeting in the world opened on 22 August 1909 on a small racecourse near the city of Reims in France. In the four-and-a-half years since the Wright brothers' triumph the advances in aircraft and their engines had been dramatic, as would be demonstrated in air races and displays. The event was sponsored by leading champagne houses, and a city of wood and canvas was erected, including a special railway station and innumerable restaurants, florists, a hairdresser, a shoeshine parlour and a large telephone/telegraph installation with special direct lines to various capital cities. The setting for the week-long display of the leading edge of aviation could be compared to Royal Ascot.

Bleriot displayed three types from his stable, including his record-breaking Type XI. But the most revolutionary advance was the appearance of the rotary engine – which Bleriot did not adopt until November of the following year. The 'Gnome' rotary power plant, a design by the French brothers Seguin, was one of the greatest single advances in the whole field of powered flight. Prior to its invention, aircraft depended on modified internal combustion engines as used in motor cars. The Seguins concept was a fixed crankshaft around which the cylinders rotated, giving much more efficient cooling, thereby solving the major problem of engine failure due to overheating. The cylinders whirled around giving a desirable 'flywheel' effect, which produced an even torque and smoother running. However, at take-off the disadvantage of the torque effect was in maintaining a straight run. The propeller and cylinders spun around the fixed crankshaft, which was hollow and delivered petrol and oil via a pump. Castor oil was the lubricant because it does not mix with petrol, but the oil was shot out through the exhaust valves at an enormous rate. One surmises that the ingestion of castor oil was good for the pilots' digestive system! Even when special piston rings were eventually fitted, the oil consumption was still about one-quarter of that of the fuel! At the end of a flight a pilot would be heavily bespattered.

By the time Corbett Wilson got airborne, there were five different rotary engines being manufactured, three of which were Gnomes. The best of these was the seven-cylinder model developing 50 hp.

During the early months of the Great War three varieties of the Mk XI were operated by the French Army's air force – differences were mainly the power of the engines, ranging from 50 hp, via 70 hp for a two-seater, to the 140 hp Gnome that powered a three-seater version. Initially, like other warplanes, the Bleriots were unarmed, but soon they were equipped with bombs fixed externally on the fuselage sides. There was also a 'parasol' version that had its continuous wing clear of the fuselage and braced off a pylon, which provided a clearer view of the ground.

The RFC in France found their Bleriots less suitable under active service conditions than they had expected. After remaining several nights in the open, they showed signs of 'flabbiness' which were not found in other aeroplanes then in use, and consequently their performance in the air fell off noticeably. Although very satisfactory when new, the Bleriot came to be looked on as a bad machine for war service.

CHAPTER FOUR

The Challenge

War was not on CW's mind when, leaving France in June 1911, he returned to London. He now used Hendon Aerodrome, north of the city, where he met a fellow enthusiast, Damer Leslie Allen, who had recently received his wings, the Royal Aero Club's Aviator's Certificate No. 183. Allen was a Limerick man of similar age to CW; he was a junior partner in a firm of naval architects. He had gained his wings at the Bleriot Flying School at Hendon. Though a novice, he was keen to make the first flight over the Irish Sea to his homeland, and on hearing this CW became interested. Both agreed that the best route would be from Hendon via Chester to Holyhead and then across to Dublin. Allen had arranged for mechanics to be on hand at Chester who could serve both aviators. The press promoted what was a friendly race into a contest of great rivalry with a large money wager involved! The basic truth that neither man had sufficient experience to attempt such a lengthy flight went unnoticed.

The intrepid pair planned to set out in the early morning of Wednesday 17 April 1912, but high winds prevented them from getting away until the afternoon. A telegram arrived from their Chester checkpoint reporting, 'Weather clear, wind blowing south-west, 12 mph'. CW was first away, followed a couple of minutes later by Allen. The former picked up the railway line, while the latter climbed higher to 5000 feet in the hope of finding better conditions before settling for an altitude of 2000 feet. *En*

13

route, Allen lost his way and had to come down in Cheshire to pick up his bearings. Resuming his flight almost immediately, he landed at Chester racecourse to be welcomed by that city's Lord Mayor and entourage. As yet there was no sign of CW: apparently the winds had buffeted his aircraft to the extent that he dropped his compass overboard and he too was lost. He decided to land at a farm about 15 miles from Hereford, but it was now too late in the day to buy another compass. A car brought him into the town where his initial welcome was decidedly frosty. A hotel receptionist, viewing a figure clad in flying gear and without luggage, decided that there were no vacancies. CW journeyed on to the Mitre Hotel and a much more friendly welcome.

Allen, in the meantime, had no such problems and with the help of his mechanic he checked his engine, and took off secure in the knowledge that CW was delayed. Following the railway line to Holyhead, he arrived there in less than 2 hours for the 85-mile leg. He didn't land, but crowds of people saw him fly out to sea until he disappeared from view going in the direction of Ireland.

Up early, CW managed to purchase a replacement compass, together with fuel and oil. However, his mechanic did not show up until midday, by which time he had learned that his rival now had a head start. He provisionally booked another night at his hotel but by late afternoon he got away to the cheers of a large crowd. Chester was less than 100 miles away – but another problem arose. The lubricating oil proved to be the wrong grade and he had to land again, high up in the Welsh mountains. In his own words:

> There I had an escape from smashing, as when the motor started missing – and really badly missing too – I was 1200 metres over the hills and saw nothing for it but to come down onto the fields at a steep angle which should have proved disastrous. However, by the greatest luck I managed

to get down on the only level bit of ground for miles, only 120 yards long and about 40 wide and well fenced.

He had been extremely lucky, but he was to be delayed for a further three days in the little village of Colva while his mechanic arrived with the proper grade of lubricant and extra supplies of fuel.

But now Allen seemed to be in trouble. The Bleriot representative in London worriedly said, 'We have received no news as to the presence of Mr. Allen. If he were found anywhere I should have been informed at once, but so far I have not heard a word from him'. It was hoped that if he had come down in the sea he could have been picked up by a vessel, but after a couple of days without news it was obvious that the Irish Sea had claimed him. He had neglected to equip himself with a cork lifebelt, and his general lack of planning was highlighted in *Flight* magazine thus: 'It certainly seems that it is our sad lot to mourn another British life sacrificed – we think again quite unnecessarily – in the practising of the sport'. Shortly thereafter *The Times* reported that a wheel, very likely from his aircraft, had been washed up, but no further traces of man or machine were ever found.

Meanwile, waiting at Colva, CW changed his plans and decided to make his sea crossing from Fishguard. Perhaps he had been influenced by the uncertainty of Allen's fate and decided that the new course would reduce the dangerous oversea leg considerably. Arriving at the ferry port, he said, 'I had a lovely flight over moor and mountain to the sea at Goodwick'. Here, he waited for his mechanic to catch up with him and give the aircraft a thorough servicing. It had taken him five days to reach his revised jumping-off point.

CHAPTER FIVE

The Crossing

At six in the morning on a mild April day CW left Fishguard and headed westwards. Perfect weather attended him until he was 15 miles from Ireland and then, as he later reported:

> I ran into a squall, wind and rain and most unpleasant; whatever height I tried, it was bad. After about 30 minutes of it the motor began to miss; the compass was also behaving erratically and visibility was bad. I had difficulty in keeping my course.

Everything seemed to be combining to bring him down but:

> as it happened I was near land and soon got a glimpse of fields. I staggered on for another ten miles with a failing engine and, just two miles from Enniscorthy, I decided to come down. It was still pouring when I landed and the machine was saturated. The landing chassis was somewhat damaged in this encounter with a good honest Wexford stone-faced bank. I landed in fog and didn't realize the field was so small till too late. However, very little damage is done.

The propeller had been broken and the undercarriage damaged but CW was intact – despite landing in that Irish phenomenon:

a combination of rain and fog! His record crossing had been accomplished in 1 hour and 40 minutes. CW had proved that there is some sense in the Irish country saying: 'The longest way round, is the shortest way home'!

The pioneer's progress had been watched with mounting excitement by all of Co. Kilkenny, and when the good news came from Wexford that he had arrived there safely, jubilation was unbounded. The British and Irish newspapers were loud in their praise. London's *Evening Standard* maintained that 'Mr. Corbett-Wilson's flight over the Irish Channel is one of the finest achievements of aviation'. Another paper referred to him as being, 'A member of a well-known Kilkenny family'. Although the major news item that April was the *Titanic* disaster, CW's exploits received a considerable amount of coverage by the press. One nationalist magazine *Irish Freedom* was quick to claim him as, 'one of our own' and published the following comment in June:

> Since we last wrote, the Irish Sea has been for the first time crossed in an aeroplane, and by an Irishman. It is gratifying that the first big flight to this country should be by a native pilot, and that we have not (as the mighty Anglo-Saxon race across the Channel had) to look to outsiders for the first attempts at mastery of the air within our boundaries. In this connnection, it is interesting to note that when Mr. Corbett-Wilson, as a new and comparatively inexperienced hand at the game, announced his intention of flying from Fishguard to Ireland, the English Press, no doubt assuming that he would be lost on the way, made no concealment of his nationality. He was simply a foolhardy Kilkenny man. The morning after his arrival in Enniscorthy all was different. It was the 'latest triumph of British aviation'. Tis thus we serve the Empire!

Despite his adventures, on the following day our hero attended Puncherstown Races, a major fixture and social event in the racing calendar.

Unknown to Corbett Wilson he had just beaten a rival by a few days.

CHAPTER SIX

Another Rival: Vivian Hewitt

Early in April 1912 a telegram arrived at the Station Hotel in Holyhead; it read: 'Do not start in wind or fog/let me know when/Mother'. This message could well have been from Corbett Wilson's worried mother, but in fact it was directed to another individual, Vivian Hewitt, who was hard on the heels of CW in the race to be first across the Irish Sea.

Hewitt, like CW, had the resources to indulge in racing cars and aeroplanes, having learnt something about flying from his own full-sized home-built gliders – and later at Brooklands in 1909. The family money came from a thriving brewery, Hewitt Brothers Ltd of Grimsby – though the family was Welsh. One of Vivian's more gentle pursuits was bird watching and ornithology generally, but it is unlikely that this provoked his urge to fly!

But to get back to the telegram. At the beginning of 1910 Hewitt had invested £1100 in a Bleriot XI, which he collected from Pau, as had CW. Unlike Corbett Wilson, due to bad weather, Hewitt was not able to take advantage of the free flying lessons that went with every purchase, but he thought his basic training at Brooklands Flying School in South London would enable him to get his new acquisition home. However, during take-off his engine stopped and he crashed into a hedge, damaging the 'frame' – the Bleriot's rudimentary fuselage.

Eventually, he got back to Brooklands to a scolding from his mother: 'You are now 23, the age at which a man should be putting his mind to marriage and a home, not concentrating on motor cars and these new-fangled flying machines'. This did not deter him.

Some two years later Hewitt's mother was still worried – as per the telegram. During those years he had become obsessed with being the first to fly across the Irish Sea and was now positioned at Rhyl for that very adventure. This was during the actual week that Leslie Allen and CW were to make an attempt: Hewitt despaired of being the first until the evening papers carried the headline 'Airman lost in Irish Sea' – this referred to the unfortunate Leslie Allen. Unaware of Corbett Wilson's success on the Tuesday, Hewitt took off for Dublin on the Friday. He made it to the Phoenix Park as planned, still thinking he was the first across.

Two years later, the Great War broke out. Unable to satisfy the medical standards for active service with the Royal Flying Corps (RFC), Hewitt nevertheless secured a commission in the Royal Naval Volunteer Reserve and was posted to America as a test pilot for the Curtiss Aircraft Company, which was manufacturing aircraft for the Allies. Like Corbett Wilson, Vivian Hewitt was a kind and gentle man; he never married but was very close to his extended family. After the war he lived in Nassau before eventually returning to Wales and his other passion for ornithology and the preservation of bird life. He died peacefully in 1964 at his old family home.

CHAPTER SEVEN

In Irish Skies

C orbett Wilson's aircraft required some minor repairs after the crossing. These were carried out at a local garage in Enniscorthy before he flew it back to Darver House on a fine Sunday morning. Parishioners were making their way to Mass in Fethard, Co. Tipperary, when they spotted CW aloft. He became completely lost, apparently because his compass had been knocked about during the sea crossing, so he decided to land in order to pick up his bearings. He came down in a field owned by Mrs Henry Quinn, just 4 miles from the town. In the words of a local reporter:

> Needless to say, in a district where the nearest railway station was many miles away, and the shriek of a steam engine had never been heard, the unexpected arrival of an aeroplane caused quite a sensation. In a very short time a huge crowd had gathered and all day long a continuous stream of people came to see the 'flying man' and his marvellous machine.

After being hospitably entertained throughout the day, from 8 a.m. to 6 p.m., CW continued his journey and landed safely at his home an hour later. Home was close to the polo grounds at Ardaloo where he based the Bleriot.

The next day he made an unannounced flight circling Kilkenny City at 500 feet; the word soon got around and long

23

KILCASH SPORTS

SUNDAY, SEPTEMBER 1st, 1912.

Come in your Thousands

AND SEE

MR. CORBETT WILSON,

THE DARING IRISH AVIATOR,

Fly over the Golden Vale beneath the Shadows of Historic
SLIEVENAMON.

Programme of Events :

1	300 yards Boy's Race, (under 16 years)	7	3 Miles Bicycle Race, (open)
2	100 yards [open] handicap	8	Tug-of-War for two aside, (open)
3	100 yards for boys under 10 years,	9	5 Miles Bicycle Race, (open)
4	440 yards [open]	10	Tug-of-War for 6 aside (open)
5	Half Mile do.		(out to exceed 60 stone)
6	One Mile do. handicap	11	5 Miles Marathon Race (open) handicap
		12	Dancing Competition (open)

Entry for each Event, 1s.   General Entry, 2s. 6d.
Entrance Fee must accompany each entry. Entries close
with Hon. Secs. on THURSDAY, 29th August.

VALUABLE PRIZES WILL BE GIVEN.

PATRICK RYAN, Kilcash,
J. LONERGAN, do. HON. SECS.

Sports commence at 12-30. Admission to Grounds, 4d.

before he was due to take off hundreds of spectators had gathered at Ardaloo. This was the beginning of an intensive series of flights and displays and CW could rightly claim to have popularised flying, or 'aeroplaning' as it was called in the early days, in the south and east of Ireland. All proceeds from his well-attended displays went to various charities – another measure of the man.

When he made a return trip to his landfall at Enniscorthy, special trains brought large numbers to see their hero in action. A few days later he gave a display at Ardaloo, which was attended by huge crowds amid a garden party atmosphere. Amongst the crowd there was a 'conman' offering genuine copies of Vivian Hewitt's autograph: this 'memento' of CW's rival was snapped up because aviation had become the current craze.

A local 'poet' had the distinction of having his doggerel published in full by *The Aeroplane* – one stanza will suffice here:

Long life to Mr. Wilson, may his courage never fail;
May a hundred years pass over ere his coffin needs a nail;
May the God above protect him, and bring him safely
    through,
To give us all another show some day at Ardaloo!

His reputation as a skilful, daring aviator and his general popularity was now so high that the City of Kilkenny organised a presentation to him. This took the form of a magnificent silver model of his Bleriot. The inscription read 'Presented to Denys Corbet Wilson, Esq., Darver, Kilkenny by some of his friends in the City and County of Kilkenny as a tribute of admiration for skill and daring as the first aviator who flew from Britain to Ireland. December 1912'. The presentation was made by the Very Rev. Dean Winder. Accepting it, CW said that it was a delightful gift and would be treasured in his house, to be handed down to his children and his children's children – when he was in the proud position of having any! This splendid trophy was eventually to find its way to the nascent Irish Aviation Museum at Dublin Airport.

Later, slight damage sustained by the Bleriot caused a planned display at Clonmel, the capital of Co. Tipperary, to be postponed – but on the rearranged date bigger trouble awaited. Despite foggy conditions, he arrived at the venue, Powerstown Park Racecourse but on his approach he failed to spot a patch of uneven ground and crashed heavily. He reported: 'As a result of the impact my face was cut under the right eye by the corner of the compass frame which smashed one of my lenses [of his goggles]. However I am lucky in having escaped so well'. His aircraft did not escape: its propeller and undercarriage were broken, the fuselage twisted, and the engine severely damaged. Despite his injuries and the damage to his machine, his main concern was for the disappointed crowd: 'But it is such a pity! – and such a beautiful day too . . . . Ah, it is too bad, too bad!'. The machine was sent back to the Bleriot works at Buc near Paris for a complete rebuild.

CW promised to return to Clonmel and in due course he gave an excellent display there.

CHAPTER EIGHT

CW Joins Up

While the Bleriot was being repaired, CW seized the opportunity to continue flying at the expense of His Majesty, King George V. In April 1912 the Royal Flying Corps had been formed and July saw CW offering himself for service. The old debate between heavier-than-air and lighter-than-air machines for military purposes had not yet been completely resolved. However, powered aeroplanes held exciting potential, primarily as cavalry of the air – though this was only realised very gradually.

The new RFC had two divisions, a Military Wing and a Naval Wing and it was to the former that Corbett Wilson presented himself; with his substantial military background and as a fully qualified pilot he was an obviously welcome recruit. Other military and naval applicants had to qualify for the Aero Club Certificate, at their own expense, but leave-of-absence to obtain this was readily granted. On satisfying the RFC, this expenditure was repaid. Military thinking had moved fairly quickly since 1908 when a distinguished general had insisted that aerial observation was a futile concept. Nevertheless, some officers, even those up to the age of 40, were learning to fly. One of these, Brigadier-General Henderson, was a moving spirit. He had written a book on 'The Art of Reconnaissance' which clearly demonstrated the future of the aeroplane in scouting operations, traditionally the province of the cavalry. He had observed the

French Army exercises in 1910 and his vision was reinforced by what he witnessed during these.

Initially, the RFC's Military Wing was to have 133 qualified officers who would learn military flying at the newly established Central Flying School. The unit in which CW would eventually serve was No. 3 Squadron, which had been formed from No. 2 (Aeroplane) Company, Air Battalion, Royal Engineers, thus becoming the premier RFC squadron on 13 May 1912. This unit experimented with balloons before the age of powered flight had dawned in 1903, and thereafter included an Air Company to examine the new technique.

As an experienced pilot and a Reservist, CW's military duties seem to have been virtually non-existent, and he arranged to be released *pro tem* to collect his newly repaired aircraft in Paris. He made several flights throughout September and returned leisurely to Farnborough, though not without incident. From Paris he had flown via Dieppe to Calais and thence across the Channel where shortage of fuel caused him to land in Sussex. He was feared missing and his obituary was written in some newspapers, but these were somewhat premature as later it was learned that bad weather had caused him to change course.

At Farnborough CW took part in official RFC trials and military exercises. One of the lessons learnt was that with good visibility the ground troops could be observed from altitudes of at least 6000 feet. Two fatalities, one before the trials and another during the manoeuvres, caused the RFC to ban all monoplanes. At the end of the Army exercises the RFC squadrons came together at Netheravon and after this debriefing CW departed to keep an appointment at Waterford.

He flew in his own machine from Farnborough to Fishguard and, aided by a tail wind, he covered the 220 miles in two-and-a-half hours. At the packet-boat port he considered having his plane crated and shipped back to Ireland as the weather was particularly bad. But on second thoughts he took off and had made the sea crossing before a misfiring engine forced him down at Gorey in north Wexford. He eventually arrived home at Darver four days after leaving Farnborough.

CHAPTER NINE

European Adventures

U ntroubled by military duties, the beginning of the New Year saw CW return to his *alma mater* at Pau. By April he had visited the Bleriot factory and invested in a new aircraft, this time a two-seater Type XI-2. He made several flights in the vicinity of Paris with his mother accompanying him. Another occasional passenger was Loftus Bryan, a lieutenant in the South Irish Horse and CW's neighbour in Kilkenny. No doubt these flights influenced this officer to join the RFC later.

On the Continent, CW's reputation as a long-distance flyer was well known and he was now about to enhance it when, accompanied by a mechanic, Potet, he took off from Buc and after three hours landed at Dijon. He stated: 'I am on the way to see Nicole at Vevey'. Leaving Dijon, the pair flew to Lausanne where CW was the guest of honour at a reception. He had crossed the Jura Alps and flown 270 miles. The press was loud in its praise and there were many tributes to 'L'inglese Wilson Corbete', 'Der englische Flieger Corbete Wilson' and 'L'excellent sportsman anglais, Monsieur Corbett Wilson'. CW was very impressed with Lausanne: 'This is the most heavenly spot' he said as he gave many joyrides over the surrounding area.

On the last day of May 1913, the pair left Lausanne (it is not clear if he kept a *rendezvous* with Nicole) with the intention of flying via Dover to Hendon, but the weather had other ideas and he had to put down at Langres, and it was not until 12 June that he could leave there though the wind was still contrary. They eventually arrived at Amiens and Potet swore that at times they had been going backwards! They pressed on to Boulogne and flew the 120-mile leg to Hendon in an hour-and-a-quarter. For the rest of the month CW spent a congenial time in the south of England visiting friends and flying across the Solent to the Isle of Wight. Here he gave many displays, which were supported, as usual, by large crowds of cheering spectators.

CW had been booked to attend the Waterford Agricultural Show on 16 and 17 July and he embarked on this long flight, causing great excitement at Wells where he made a short stop. His next stop near Bristol was unscheduled when, hampered by poor visibility, he crashed. His Bleriot was severely damaged but neither he nor his mechanic were badly hurt. He was able to borrow the two-seater Bleriot owned by the intrepid Miss Trehawke Davies. This lady had agreed to fly with him in Waterford but due to illness gave up her seat to an *Irish Times* reporter. On the first day of the display CW casually told the newspaperman: 'By the way, whatever happens, you will sit tight, won't you?' But as they taxied out the aircraft struck a rut, which removed the propeller tips. The ever-efficient Bleriot Company at Hendon sent a special messenger with a new propeller who arrived next day. The reporter readily gave up his seat to CW's friend Loftus Bryan, and everything proceeded smoothly thereafter. At the end, CW was carried shoulder high around the grounds to a great ovation.

Corbett Wilson stayed at his home but in late October he resigned his commission in the RFC. He gave up the lease on Darver House and sold up his stable of horses. Perhaps after four years in Ireland he felt it was time for a move; certainly he had now given up his expensive hobby in the air. The news was greeted with dismay by the local population who regarded him as 'one of our own' – the highest accolade!

Perhaps wanderlust and the challenge of a new setting enticed the Corbett Wilsons to a new home. They leased Villa D'Este on the shores of beautiful Lake Como in northern Italy where they led an idyllic life. CW was no longer airborne, but was enjoying himself by disturbing the tranquillity of the lake by racing speedboats on its broad reaches. But political troubles in the Balkans were boiling over and culminated in the outbreak of the Great War. The call to arms immediately changed the life of this lotus-eater.

As the following letters show, CW could not wait to get back to the RFC and be sent on active service. This was the enthusiastic period when every young man wanted to 'do his bit' over in France. The pundits said, 'it will all be over by Christmas' and no man of spirit wanted to miss the fun! Disillusionment had yet to set in.

Leaving his mother in the care of their faithful retainer Pietro, CW was on his way to rejoin the RFC – a journey recorded in the following letters.

CHAPTER TEN

The RFC Flies
Off to War

War was declared on 4 August and on 11 August the
RFC headquarters unit left Farnborough for France
– its motor transport having preceded it. The headquarters incorporated 'The Aircraft Park', which was in effect a
travelling base for all the squadrons, with twenty aircraft
allotted to it. The Park was the nucleus of a vast supply and
maintenance system, and three days after its arrival was located
at Le Havre. When the early German advance threatened this
site, the Park moved to St Omer, which became its permanent
base for the early years of the war.

From 13 to 15 August the four operational squadrons, a total
of 163 aircraft, roared off from the Downs above Dover, No. 3
Squadron suffering a fatal accident to one of its Bleriots at the
onset while taking off to position at Dover. Apart from one flight
left behind for coastal patrol duties and training, these planes
represented the entire strength of British military aviation. By 17
August, the squadrons had moved up to the Front at airfields
near Maubeuge, where they stayed grounded for two days with
100 frustrated pilots cursing the bad visibility, which ruled out
reconnaissance.

The unit in which Corbett Wilson was to serve for all of his
time in France was No. 3 Squadron – the 'premier' squadron.
The unit had been well blooded before CW caught up with it in

35

October. On its formation it was equipped with BEs and Farmans, but by the outbreak of the Great War in August 1914, under the command of Major J.M. Salmond, it had an inventory of seven Bleriots, four Henri Farmans, and a BE. It flew to France in August with the other squadrons.

Witnessing the Munster Fusiliers advancing to confront the enemy at Mons, one of the pilots commented: 'We were rather sorry they had come up because till then we had only been fired on by the French!' One pilot had already been shot down by his own side but had survived. Despite the Union flags painted on the underside of wings, troops fired first and rarely asked questions afterwards; this did not enamour them to the pilots who were swearing, dodging, swerving and climbing briskly out of harm's way. Of course, it was not easy in sunlight to distinguish between the crosses on the Union flag and the black crosses of the Germans. This led to the introduction of 'roundels': blue/white/red at the centre for the RFC, the colours reversed from the French roundels.

A Bleriot of No. 3 Squadron carried out the first reconnaissance on the 19 August. Aerial reconnaissance came into its own straight away and this sortie, and others that followed, made a major contribution to saving the BEF (British Expeditionary Force) from encirclement and destruction by the advancing German Armies. On 22 August reconnaissance clearly showed this impending disaster, which initiated 'The Retreat From Mons'. At first light on that day Capt. Shephard and Lt Bonham-Carter, airborne in an Avro 504, spotted that the German right flank was turning to encompass the BEF. To report back to their squadron with this crucial news was difficult because it was on the move to Le Cateau.

As the airmen scoured the area, hedgehopping to avoid ground fire and blinded by smoke from burnt-out villages, they eventually spotted a bright red delivery van, part of their squadron's commandeered transport column. This flight was typical of the reconnaissance missions, which allowed the retreating BEF to keep one jump ahead of the enemy's steady advance.

Aerial reconnaissance was carried out continually and its value was inestimable for the BEF commanders. It could be claimed that RFC intelligence saved the BEF because a cavalry screen would undoubtedly have been brushed aside by the Germans, and it is very doubtful if cavalry could have assessed the strength of the enemy and got this information quickly back to headquarters. Unfortunately, many high-ranking commanders were often incredulous and unenthusiastic about the information the airmen delivered. This would change.

During the retreat there was a catastrophic change in the weather for a time. The fliers could barely see the ground through rain-spattered goggles and sweeping mists. At their aerodromes, the storm picked up aircraft from the ground, tossed them high in the air and hurled them back to earth in fragments. One morning the RFC had a mere ten serviceable machines, but still continued to reconnoitre from its hastily patched-up planes. Personnel were moving like gypsies around France, sleeping wherever they could – in barns and chateaux, under lorries and hedgerows, but occasionally in hotels! Every day aircrews spent many hours in the air searching for the enemy – and half as long again searching for their bases. There was no guarantee that the makeshift bases from which they had taken off would still be available when they returned to the fields. On one occasion, a couple of officers flew to Paris for spare parts and then back to their Mess only to find German officers dining where they had taken breakfast!

The retreat was very hard on the troops. A Tommy (who was later awarded the VC) described the rout: 'It was a 200 mile slog in merciless heat, always within range of German fire. We had not a single day's rest: when we were not fighting we were marching as hard as we could'. The retreat ended on 9 September and after the Allied victory at the Battle of the Marne a static front was established. No. 3 Squadron could proudly boast that it had not abandoned or lost an aircraft or a vehicle during the retreat, and had fewer than half-a-dozen crashes on the fourteen temporary aerodromes it had occupied as the RFC drew back.

The crucial part played by the airmen throughout the retreat, and the battle which followed, did not go unrecognised. The BEF Commander-in-Chief stated:

> I wish particularly to bring to notice the admirable work done by the Royal Flying Corps under Sir David Henderson. The airmen's skill, energy and perseverance have been beyond all praise. They have furnished me with the most complete and accurate information which has been of incalculable value in the conduct of operations. Fired at constantly by friend and foe, and not hesitating to fly in every kind of weather, they have remained undaunted throughout.

Now static trench warfare called for aerial co-operation very different, and at least as dangerous as the preceding war of movement. Two pairs of squadrons were now formed into the 1st and 2nd Wings, each supporting a specific Army Corps with No. 3 Squadron in the latter Wing. Artillery observation – spotting targets and the fall of shot – was a prime duty, which involved the constant problem of rudimentary communications. Wireless-equipped aircraft were few at first so other forms of signalling, lamps and Very flares, had to be used. Eventually the advantage of wireless over these uncertain methods prompted a Corps Commander to report:

> Today I watched for a long time an aeroplane observing for the 6 inch howitzers of the Third Division. It was, at times, smothered with hostile anti-aircraft guns, but nothing daunted, it continued for hours through a wireless installation to observe the fire and indeed to control the battery, with most satisfactory results.

The war on the Western Front now settled into a long drawn out stalemate, but while the opening round was being fought Corbett Wilson was doing everything he could to get back to Farnborough.

CHAPTER ELEVEN

Letters: 13 August to 4 November 1914

Paris
13th August, 1914

Dearest Mother,

Only just got here, such a journey, but with all the discomfort it was rather fun. I met some charming people and we made merry, sometimes in 1st class carriages, sometimes in second, wherever we could get. All the trains are full to the heads and they crawl along stopping everywhere: and the heat! However I'm here. I leave again tomorrow for England. We met a constant stream of troop trains going back. News is good if to be believed. I think I tried to telegraph before, but you have to go to the Mairie [Town Hall] and there are all sorts of formalities. I hope mine gets through. They say there is a great battle in progress, it's all very exciting.

All the trains going last had pictures of William [Kaiser Wilhelm II] in various guises, mostly pigs with helmets on and fierce moustaches. All bridges and level crossings, in fact the whole line is guarded by infantry.

We saw one train entirely composed of Hotel motor buses [presumably on flat cars] and right in front of our carriages was the big Hotel du Palais 'Bus de Biarritz'. At one station the train was full, and there on the platform were 300 people all wanting to get in. In the end our train was miles long from constant additions.

Must stop, best love; going to dinner; our meals were somewhat scrappy in the train.

Love from
D.

Paris is a desert, all shops shut, also Castiglione. The Italian papers are fairly reliable, but news is scarce.

NOTE: Italy maintained its neutrality until it joined the Allies in May 1915.

Hans Crescent Hotel,
Belgravia,
London, S.W.
15th August, 1914

Dearest Mother,

Got in here last night after really a quite nice journey considering all things. The heat was bad in France, and we had to change continually, still we were very lucky, and always got seats, and at Dijon, myself and three others couldn't get on the connecting train as it was quite full, not even standing room, so we waited till three o'clock in the morning and managed to get two 2nd class to ourselves, so that we got a whole length of carriage each.

We had to stop to fly off to Waterloo for a train as they thought one went almost at once. however [sic], I've got an hour to wait, so am having some breakfast.

In train. The news is good, everything seems to be going well, and yesterday we saw a huge transport come into Boulogne full of our troops, mostly Highlanders, and off Dover were the watch-dogs, six huge men-of-war.

They seemed to have secured safety for the merchant service.

The Belgians still hold all the forts round Liege. I came through from Modane with a Belgian hospital nurse, a charming person. She was going direct to the front. One of her brothers was in one of the forts before Liege.

Lord Kitchener's scheme seems good; he proposes to raise an army of 100,000 for the War only, some to go abroad after six months training, others to stay in England. Only those who have no ties to go abroad, and not till a certain efficiency is obtained, the most efficient corps to have the honour of going first, to Belgium or anywhere. The whole of this army is to be disbanded at peace. I am wondering what they will do with me. However I'm at Woking now, quite near, so shall know, I hope, soon. Will finish this later.

17th August.
Well, I got to Farnboro' and was told that I must first see the War Office man. I was given a letter of introduction to him and saw him this morning. He was very nice and said yes I was wanted. He sent me to a doctor who examined me, all right. Then he said could I join at once? I said Could I not? Well, I am to go and join Wednesday morning. I have to try and get some kit first, a coat and trousers, then I'm off to Farnboro'. He says there will be 20 Bleriots soon. I told him I was laughed at for suggesting Bleriots two years ago, and he laughed and said he knew. He also said that perhaps I could go with the next draft for Belgium or France. I said I was desperately keen to go and asked him to put in a word for me. He said he would do his best, but that the Major had already done so.

NOTE: When CW eventually arrived at Farnborough he was more impressed than had he gone to the Central Flying School at Upavon. The operational squadrons had taken 105 officers, 755 other ranks, and 63 aircraft to France. This left 163 aircraft at the CFS – but only 20 of the latter were fit for training purposes, the remainder were destined for the scrap heap.

Barrington Kenett has already gone to Belgium, also fifty machines and pilots, but all is very secret and no one knows anything; even the troops have no idea where they are going.

I lunched today with the Heydemans. They are sad, poor things, they may lose all their money owing to German investments. Also one son has just gone to the war with the Queen's Bays. Nicole looked pale, and was not very cheerful, poor dear.

I also when at Farnboro' had time to go to see the Peytons. I thought perhaps the General might help me. I saw "Naughty" who looked blooming. She sent much love. The General has been sent to command at Bury St. Edmunds, just a country command. N. said he was furious at not getting a war job, naturally. Then 'pire en pire' [worse upon worse] the 15th have been divided up for what is called divisional cavalry and their poor commander is not even allowed to take his regiment into action. This seems silly, but everyone seems glad that Kitchener is at Whitehall. I am content so far, but hope indeed that I may get away with this next draft.

The Germans seem to be in a very queer fix; how they are to extricate themselves seems to me to be a problem which is going to take some solving. Kitchener thinks that the war should last a year. He doesn't seem to have done much for Peyton [the General above]. He seemed rather to think that he had been stuffed away, which does seem so; as he seemed such an active and capable soldier. Still maybe we shall all get there, sooner or later.

News is very scarce, but everyone agrees that there must be a very big battle soon, the biggest the world has ever known, but I can't see how it can take place for a least ten days. Russia is steadily coming up, with literally millions.

Someone wrote to the paper yesterday saying the Germans had better remember that the Cossacks were at their door, and to think twice about committing these atrocities, as the Cossacks were sure to take many reprisals for each German atrocity. Naughty said the General had not had my letter, so I fear this may never get you, still it's worth trying.

The Territorials are up in great force and London is full of them, every day troops are leaving for the front. After all it's a stirring time, it will wake everyone up, and finish the German menace once and for all. It has come at a good time for us, and the wonderful Belgian resistance has checked the Germans, so that now France is quite ready for all contingencies. You in Italy get more news, I really believe than we in London, but everyone is warned of false news, especially German; they do it to keep Germany's heart up. The French news is fairly reliable.

I will go to the office and failing seeing Uncle C. will go to the bank to arrange about the money.

Yesterday it poured with rain, but today is fine; the train that brought me back from Farnboro' was three hours late, and I came here in the Guard's van; train after train of empties coming back from Southampton thundered past, going to London for more troops. Each time we thought it was our's, and each time troop train, and for three blessed hours I sat in that station. They are stirring times, and one can't help feeling very elated, though, or course, it's all very terrible. They say the Germans are doing what I told you they would, trying to take the positions by weight of numbers, and their losses are naturally terrible. They are short of food, and I believe very sick of it already.

Well, I hope you are all right and that all goes well. Wire to me c/o Royal Flying Corps, South Farnborough, Hants, if you want to know anything.

Best of love to you. I will wire you whenever anything important happens to me.

Ever your loving,
DEN

NOTE: The enthusiasm and the pathetic anxiety to see action in the early days "before it was all over" seemed very poignant in later years.

The Farnborough Queen's Hotel,
South Farnborough.
19th August, 1914

Dearest Mother,

Here I am. I got down this morning. I was to have taken out one of the 50hp Bleriots, but alas both their motors are in bits for overhaul! They say they'll be ready tomorrow, in the meanwhile I must wait, they've already sent out a lot of machines to France, and still have a good many here, mostly biplanes. There's lots doing and everyone seems very busy, and much better run than of old, [CW would know from his earlier service in the newly formed RFC] still that's only natural, as they've been at it more than 2 years. I don't know anyone here yet, much, and just kicking about isn't very amusing, still I hope I shall get going tomorrow. Practically none of the people I knew are here now. I saw Valentine today, he's at the same job as I. You remember he was at Pau.

I hear Loftus Bryan [his neighbour in Kilkenny] is in the Corps somewhere, but haven't traced him yet. The car would be invaluable, I wish I had it here. Write to me here in c/o RFC as I told you, this place is the RFC mess.

I went to the Office but did not see Uncle C. though Uncle John and Alfred were there and told me they had £100 for me, and that they had sent you £110 or £150 so that's all right. Alfred came to dinner with me. Uncle John looked blooming. I bought some camp kit, etc., not much, just the bare necessities. The new Bleriot's [sic] that the War Office man told me of are not yet delivered unfortunately, and no one seems to know when they will be, still I may get put on a Morane. [There were a few early types at Farnborough] News is good so far though the censor is very strict [this is hard to believe when one considers the amount of information in CW's letters] and we only get very little through. We've only just heard that the expeditionary force has landed, when I knew it more than a week ago in France. It's a good thing all the same, as the whole force was put into France and no one knew where they were and how they got there – all nicely baffling for the German spies. Now we shall be without news again for some time. Liege is apparently occupied by the Germans, but the forts still hold on, though they are now cut off. The French continue to advance in Alsace. The reports that Garros [the noted French pilot] had flown into a German dirigible [Zeppelin airship] and smashed it up and himself is quite untrue as far as I can make out. We have many such reports, and it's a great chance for mystery makers. General Grierson who was to have commanded one of the Army Corps for the front died suddenly in a train. A man who I was dining with yesterday said he was certain he'd been shot by a German spy, as he, Grierson, was much feared by the Germans as he knew a great deal about them and their tactics. This chap said it was ridiculous to say that a man in Grierson's position, just off to the front, and of course passed by all doctors, had died from heart [problems]. It certainly does seem queer. Then also they say that we had artillery in the defence of Liege,

though this I don't in the least believe. You can make your
mind easy about news, you get all and more we get here; so
much that things I knew before leaving Como are first
news here. General French is commanding on land and
Jellicoe the N. Sea. I've had a rare go of indigestion, but am
better today and hope it's departed. I was very lucky to get
in here, as it's full of RFC and one had to take one's chance
of a room or go out into the town, there is no camp.

Well bye bye for now. With much love.

Ever your loving,

DEN.

You could send on any letters if you like, I think they'd get
here.

The Farnborough Queen's Hotel,
South Farnborough.
20th August, 1914

My Dearest Mother,

Well I've started again with varied success. I went out first
three times on the Bleriot just to see how I felt after a year's
absence. That was all right. I felt quite right on her. Then I
was put on to the Morane 80 h.p. the little monoplane that
all the records have been done with in France. Garros
"flied" this one. Well I loved it in the air, it was perfect, so
steady, just delightful, but on landing I misjudged the
sloping ground and buckled a wheel and damaged just the
tip of the wing, the machine will be ready again this
evening, so little damage was done thank heavens, still it
was stupid but the machine has a very bad reputation for
its landing capabilities and I think this made me land

differently from usual as I was trying to allow against its said propensity for turning over. However, this morning I did better and landed twice all right. I love the machine, it's very fast and very steady, and should be of immense use in the war, owing to its speed and it's nicer than the 80hp Bleriot, unfortunately there are only 4 and they've no prospect of getting more. I do want to get out to the front, but they tell me it will be all a month before they send more. I rather wish I had joined France [the French Air Force] as then it would have been a certainty I suppose, as it is I must consider myself lucky to have got in the Morane as it is without doubt the best machine there is, and here the pilots are rather shy of it, owing to the said difficulty of landing. In France also the military pilots don't like them for much the same reason, that you have not much chance in a small field, but I hope with practice to get over a lot of the initial difficulty. I hope you are going on all right, and that you get my letters. I've had nothing from you yet. If you find you want to come home, I think I could get away for a week for that, then you could come here and stay till we see what's doing. This Colonel man here seems a good chap. I tackled him again about going out to France and he said we must all wait, everyone wanted to get there and that he had the worst job of all as he saw no prospect, but had to sit down here and run the thing. He said we'd all get our turn, but it's the first people who will have the most interesting time. However, I can't do more, and am fairly started, [on his refresher flying] hedged round with Captains and Military ways!!
Best of love to you, let me know soon how things are.
DEN.
News is good.
P.S. They say the occupation of Brussels is merely a bait and that the Germans have walked into it, but I dunno. I hope it is; of course Brussels couldn't withstand them, it's

not fortified at all, but I should like to hear that they get a good smashing soon from the Allies.

Namur can hold out indefinitely, I believe, and the Allies ought to get a knock at them soon, but I'm sure you get as much and more news than we do.

———————————

5th September, 1914

Dearest Dum
[an affectionate childhood name]
I hear postcards get through best, and so I haven't been writing letters as you only seem to get them so long after, still I'll post one same time as this and you can tell me which gets first. We are still waiting. I have no idea when we shall get away. We have only two Moranes and one Bleriot 50hp, but we are to have another Morane, then we might get away. They like to send them out in flights [rather than singly]. Weather lovely, have been flying every day. One day went to Salisbury Plains, another to Brooklands.

Everyone very nice here. I am quite enjoying life, only it seems everlasting waiting. Still I suppose we shall get off some time. No news of our aircraft. News seems slightly better tonight, but I don't like the look of it. The sea route is the only one for you now.

Love to Jock. [CW's faithful dog who would have to endure a lengthy quarantine when he eventually reached the UK.]

Don't attempt long train journeys, anyway you can't cross France now.
Hope you are much better.
Best of love,
D.

The Farnborough Queen's Hotel
South Farnborough
September 5th, 1914

Dearest Dum,

I have not been writing letters as I'd given up, as you never seem to get them till ages after.

I've written postcards and telegraphed as being better. I am enjoying life here. I've been handed over a Morane 80hp Gnome Monoplane, and I've pretty entirely the sole use of it. It's nice to have one's own machine. I fly every day, and get as much practice as I can. The C.O. said the other day 'a propos' of going to the front that I must not be down-hearted that we shall all get our turn. He's been very nice to me, but our flight is short of mechanics and machines, we can only raise two Moranes, one I fly and the other is flown by a sergeant, who was one of Graham White's professional flyers before the war. Then there is one 50hp Bleriot and one Sopwith, which is a beast of a machine and none of the military pilots will go near it. I've heard nothing as yet to do with that, I said to the C.O. I hoped he wouldn't take me off Moranes, and he said he would not. I like the machine awfully.

Bill Eyre cast up here yesterday, and today he has taken on a sergeant's job, failing a commission RFC. He's a useful mechanic.

I saw Eddie in town and he's looking for a job too. Bryan [Loftus, his neighbour in Kilkenny and a lieutenant in the South Irish Horse] I hear is soldiering in Ireland. I also saw Barron who is likewise looking for to serve his country. The news is not good, a least I don't think it is reading between the lines. Germany is coming on much too fast [The retreat from Mons]. Don't attempt to cross France in anything. I think you've done quite right. Your two expressed letters came together and unless you can get a comfy train to Naples or Genoa, and comfy boat home, stay where you are; as for the car, lock it up and leave it. It's not worth sending anyone out as it's so costly. I had a man engaged but at the eleventh hour he cried off! I was really glad for I had my doubts as to the possibility of getting you home that way. Now it's quite certain there's not the least chance of your ever getting by motor, and you only expose yourself to much discomfort and danger. As to the trains they are out of the question for you and always are. The discomfort is much more than you could think of undertaking. As long as you are comfy and not worried I should hang on where you are. I will keep you well posted as to my movements, but I begin to fear we are here for a bit yet. Macdowell came back today from taking over a machine. RFC base is astonishingly far back, I mustn't say where. He didn't give a very encouraging account, still I'm sure things will begin to go better soon.

All my love to you and don't fuss about things; take it easy and all will be well.

Ever your loving,
Den.

Love to Mr. Gobbles Jock.

The Farnborough Queen's Hotel,
South Farnborough.
8th September, 1914

Dearest Mother,

Two wires came today. I've written and wired lately saying that I think it better for you either to make up your mind to wait till you are absolutely obliged to go, or to take ship, leaving the car locked up. It is out of the question for you to attempt to cross France now, either in train or motor, and unless you can get a comfortable train and boat via Genoa or Naples, I must say I shouldn't risk a sea voyage unless in comfort, it's no use knocking yourself up, and I fear these mines. Still I hear there are none at all in your course. If you could get a steamer to Genoa or Naples and then go quietly on to the ship it would be all right, but don't risk discomfort, it will only make you ill. Uncle Julian writes he hopes you will stay on as long as you can as it's the wisest. News is much better tonight, things seems going better. I'm flying every day. I hope my letters get through, I only put in the simplest things for fear of censorship. Shall express this letter.

Best love from,
D.

If you find you must go away, you could leave the car in Genoa or Naples. Probably by then you'll have found a chauffeur.

8th September, 1914

Dearest D.

Your last wire just came, but it's quite illegible, I can make nothing of it, and will try and get it repeated. Remember to write your wire very distinctly. Was out twice today, took Dowding, my Captain, for a turn. We went out over Camberley to look for the German prisoner camp. We found it, they are in tents with barbed wire barricades

round them. No word yet as to when we go!! Still I'm
getting practice and enjoying it.
Much love, D

NOTE: Eventually, Dowding became an Air Chief Marshal and commanded
Fighter Command, RAF during the Battle of Britain – he was nicknamed
'Stuffy' because of his off-putting manner. Despite his victory in 1940, he
argued with Winston Churchill principally over Britain's later air defence and
he did not receive further employment. Nor was he elevated to the peerage
post-war, an honour he richly deserved.

Friday, 9th September, 1914

I hear P.C.'s [postcards] get through best, so here goes. I
wired you to know how you felt. I suggest that I send you
out a chauffeur. I'll go to London and find a good, reliable
man through the Automobile Association, give him an
Inter Pass, and fire him out to you. Then I should come
back by Ventimiglia and Nice, Avignon, Toulouse, Pau
and up to the Bordeaux Road to Chatres, Evreux, Rouen
and Havre. Anyway I'll find out for certain which crossing
is best and give the man all instructions.

I'm waiting your reply, but shall go London, Monday, if
don't hear, I send man out.

Was out twice today, like machine.
Best love,
D.

9th September, 1914

Dearest Dum,

B.K. and Burgie W. wrote to me from front. B.K. says RFC
is doing finely at the war, but can give me no details. B. is

on H.M.S. "Loyal" torpedo destroyer, [These vessels
eventually to be simply called 'destroyers', were then
called 'torpedo boat destroyers'] he hopes to get a smack at
the Germans. He sent you his love. He's apparently
cruising in the Channel. [On what was known as 'The
Dover Patrol'].

I fear some of my letters must have got hung up, but for
a few days when we were telegraphing I didn't write, so
perhaps all is well. The third Morane has turned up, so we
have three good machines now. I do hope they'll let me off
soon. We are doing no good here and might do something
over there. News is very cheerful, all seems going the best
now.

Hope you are feeling quite well again.

Love.

D.

Sunday, 11th September, 1914.

Dearest Mother,

Just in from a flight in the Morane. I like the machine
immensely, but there was not much doing this morning. I
was in the clouds at 1,500 feet. I find I can see the cavalry
fairly well at 6,000. It is going to be very interesting.

I'm going to London tomorrow to search for a chauffeur,
and will send him at once, with all instructions.

Think perhaps you might get home by boat from
Bordeaux, but news is not good; anyhow, I will send out
the man as a stand-by, and even if you have to leave
the car, it doesn't matter, we can get it after the war. I
am afraid you'd never stand the train, only 15 miles
an hour!

Glad to hear you are much better. Tell Grace not to worry you. Have your letter of the 22nd and at last understand why you don't get mine. Will consult the Automobile Association fully and send a long letter by chauffeur.
Love,
D.

The Farnborough Queen's Hotel,
South Farnborough.
11th September, 1914.

Dearest Dum,

Your letter dated September 1st just arrived! Express, too. Thanks for the enclosure from the French Aero Club. I am beginning to get what the soldier calls "fed up" here. It seems so futile when we have three fast monoplanes to leave them here, with always the chance of having them broken up, for nothing, when they might be doing at all events more at the front.

Trenchard, our Colonel, tells me that the authorities over there wire for the machines they require, and he has to send them off what they ask for, and as yet there has been no demand for Morane monoplanes; they've got it into their heads, I fear, that they are very hard to land, whereas with care and practice they are splendid, but they want careful handling in landing and you must land head to wind, if there is anything over 15 an hour blowing, as they have a tendency to swing round and pirouette about. They pull up after landing very quickly which is a great feature. I like the machine immensely and think it most practical for war. You get [a] very fine view out of them;

they are fast, and good flyers, and we have three good
ones, and they won't send them. I'm going up to the War
Office to agitate, it can't do any harm, and may do some
good.

The news is excellent. General French's dispatch is fine
and speaks so well of all branches of the service, and
especially well of the RFC. He says they have done
splendid work and given much good information.

We have done magnificently; the retreat was
wonderfully carried out, and all ranks have behaved well
above the standard. In fact they say the whole thing is the
most glorious in our history, – they are now advancing
and driving the Germans back over the Marne. The Ninth
Lancers have been badly cut about owing to charging over
country which held concealed machine guns, and barbed
wire. It looks like a trap. The artillery have done wonders,
both in shooting and in holding on to their positions.
Smith Dorrien was specially complimented by French for
his work in the retreat, – I must say things have turned
very much for the better. It's begun to rain here and I fear
will continue, today is very ominous-looking.

Do hope you are still carrying on all right. Wire me if
any developments crop up.

Best of love to you, D

NOTE: Hugh Trenchard, with whom CW seemed on very good terms,
reached the highest rank and became known as 'The Father of the Royal Air
Force'. His statue stands on the Embankment in London.

Monday 14th September, 1914

Dearest Mother,

I saw Uncle J. on Saturday, also W.O. [War Office] There is
nothing to do but wait patiently till we are wanted. Uncle

lunched with me, and was so nice. I think ship from Genoa is your best way. Will write fully tonight, awfully rushed now. If I could find out for sure I would not be wanted for some time I might get out and fetch you, but no one can tell.

The RFC have done splendidly, practically no casualties. Best of love, D

NOTE: In the following letter CW is so keen to see action that he considers enlisting in the French Air Force. From his training at Pau he held the French Aero Club certificate.

The Farnborough Queen's Hotel,
South Farnborough,
14th September, 1914

Dearest Dum,

I went up to the W.O. on Saturday, but got very little out of the man there, it is the old story, you will go, but we can't say when. It is rather disappointing and tiresome, however. I saw Uncle Julian also, and had a long yarn with him. He came to lunch. He suggested filling in the French Form, and if they guaranteed me a job right off, perhaps it would be worth while getting seconded to the French Service. But we came to the conclusion, that I must have a job to go to, as if not, I might fall between two stools. This is very dull apart from the flying, but it is better than 'nought'.

I wish some plan could be fixed on to get you safely home. I read your wire to uncle J but we can't advise much. I doubt the safety of France for you, though since I wrote to say – by no means attempt to cross France – things have changed for the better very considerably. I feel I could quite easily come out and get you home again before I should be wanted, but it is doubtful. They might want me and it is a long way out. Still, if I could come in uniform, I might get you through easily. I'll try and find out about that.

In the meantime, if you could get a good boat from some sea-port, I should take it and leave the car at the Villa d'Este.

The weather is very blustery and rainy here now, such a change. The Morane is good in a wind. I put in the French form that I should like to fly a Morane, to the question, "Appareil prefere" [preferred aircraft].

This place is full of all manner of soldiers, and Kitchener's New Army comes in in thousands every day. The recruiting has been wonderful. In fact the whole country has shown up in the very best light.

Don't believe any reports of our men running away. They have done marvellously, and now the Germans are in full retreat all along the line. I only wish one could have some part in it.

Best of love to you,
D

———————————

Royal Flying Corps,
Brooklands,
Byfleet.
Thursday 8th October, 1914

Dearest Mother,

I hear today that I am to take the next new 80hp Bleriot over to France. It is in the course of construction, [at the Royal Aeronautical Factory at Farnborough] and I asked today when it will be ready, and was told Monday latest.

The Squadron Commander sent for me and told me that
Colonel Trenchard had warned him that I was to take it
over. I only hope they'll stick to that. It will be lovely. I
hope to get up on Saturday or Sunday will try and wire,
anyway I'll come before I go, if go I do, it seems too good
to be true. I am very comfy here and they're charming
fellows. I flew the Morane this morning. It's much more
like business here and Longcroft is a hard worker and very
keen. [This remark seems to be in contrast to conditions at
Farnborough].

NOTE: This letter is from the Officer Commanding the RFC headquarters
which is now at Middle Wallop, Hants, one of the Corps' sites adjoining
Salisbury Plain. The letter is addressed to the Field Headquarters at St.
Omer.

Headquarters, Royal Flying Corps, M.W.
To: Officer Commanding,
    Aircraft Headquarters, Expeditionary Force.
Herewith 2/Lieut. D. Corbett Wilson on 80/Bleriot, No. —.
[the serial is omitted]
He flies a Morane equally well.

Lt. Col.
Commanding Royal Flying Corps M.W.
South Farnborough,
10th October, 1914.

———————————

Dover
16th October 1914.

Dearest Dum,

I really had quite a nice flight here. It was comparatively
clear at 2,000 feet till nearing Ashford when I had to come

down to 1,000 as fog was coming up. It was thick near here but I kept very low and found the ground quite easily. There was a wall of fog over towards London, that covered Maidstone. Very queer effect, at first I thought it was going to overtake me, but I just past [sic] it safely. The [railway] line was a great help, as it runs pretty nearly dead straight from Redhill to Folkestone. Today is misty in the Channel. I'm waiting for the car to take me to the Aerodrome, though I don't suppose I'll be let start till it clears a bit more. I took an awful time to get here. I suppose there must have been some wind against me, or else the old thing is terribly slow. The aerodrome here is right on the edge of the cliff.

I do hope I'll get on again today. I believe there is a rule that you cannot start till you can see the other side, which is absurd. I don't think they quite stick to that. I will wire on arrival. I sent two last night, one to the Queen's and the other to 3 Hans [Crescent]. Didn't know if you'd stay the night at Farnborough or go straight up.

I have a terrible fear it's getting thicker. I believe the very early morning is the best, but the car didn't come, so suppose it was thick. I hope you'll get a nice flat, I should try Cadogan Gardens. Nicoll might know of some.
Very best love to you,
From D.
[Mrs Corbett Wilson got back safely to London and was installed in an apartment in Hans Crescent, Knightsbridge].

France   19th October, 1914

Dearest Mother,

Arrived here with the machine today. We are a detached
flight camped in a farm house. I was to have gone out on
reconnaissance this afternoon but the Union Jack had to be
painted on my wings before they would let me off. We've
heard the guns all day long, there is a devil of a scrap
going on about 20 kilometres away. We are doing well.
News is good. I am off on reconnaissance tomorrow, I
hope. My machine is slow, but I hope will be improved for
the tuning up it got this afternoon. I had a very foggy
crossing, but managed to hit off Gris Nez all right, and
then I was right. Will you send me 100 cigarettes
occasionally. Freiburg Treyer, 34 Haymarket, but disguise
them as other things, send them with shirts or anything.
As I've only arrived on the scene I can't tell you much, I
will write when I can, but don't know if you'll ever get
this.

Best of love to you dearest Dum,
Ever yours,
Den.

Will you also send me some soft bedroom slippers and a
blanket and some socks for the men. Send me some forms
like this [notepaper] so I can write to you.

———————————

27th October, 1914

Dearest Dum,

I've no notepaper so as I want to send you this I'm going to write my letter on it. We've come in from our farmhouse now and are at Headquarters RFC [St. Omer]. Had the bad luck to damage my machine owing to being too heavily loaded going out on reconnaissance, I had a 14 stone observer, all tanks full, a rifle and ammunition and our heavy clothes, also the ground was bad and I had to start down wind or rather down side wind while the machine declined to fly, her tail went down and she just settled down and flopped on to one wing. However it wasn't too bad and everyone said it was quite unavoidable. We were camped out there only four miles from the firing line, and the musketry and big gun fire was pretty well continuous all day and night, but they keep changing the flights about and my flight week was up and so here we are. I'm sitting in front of a roaring campfire and have just had lunch, a sort of stew curry, very good. It's dull, foggy day and impossible for reconnaissance or nearly so, anyway they've not asked for one, so here we sit.

One of our fellows got a bullet in his plane day before yesterday, they've not done that to me yet. We seem to be somewhat of a fixture here, the ground is good and grounds north of this are hard to find, so we may stay here some time.

We have a very comfy billet outside the town, about a mile from the ground. News is good, but the Germans are holding a very strong position, and are hard to dislodge. They dig themselves in in a most wonderful way; their redoubts are splendid. Our people here are in terror of their letters being published. Please don't! [CW obviously didn't want his letters published either!]

Do get old Jock out [of quarantine] as soon as possible.
Best of love to you, dear Mother, D

———————————

Hotel Ritz,
Place Vendome,
Paris.
29th October, 1914

Dearest Dum

You'll be surprised to see this address. I've been sent down
here to get another machine for us, the life of a Bleriot is
very short at the War. I saw the machine yesterday it looks
lovely, but they are not good war machines, the one I
brought from England has been condemned as dangerous,
they found that the wood was too new and that
consequently it warped on getting damp. It got itself into
the most queer shapes. It is a waste of money buying such
stuff at all. There was quite a new machine scrapped. The
French built ones are better. The Officers of the Flying
Corps stay here for free. I've got such a nice room and
bath.

I'm going out to Buc [the Bleriot factory close to Paris]
this morning to try the machine and shall get off back to
the lines as soon as possible. I'm very well. We spend all
day on the aviation ground as you never know when
they'll want you for reconnaissance. Then we go down to
our billets for dinner and sleep. News is good as far as it
goes. It's dull and foggy today. I hope you've got a comfy
flat by now. I don't like to tell you very much about things
as I don't know what they permit, or if you'll ever get this.
I've written several times short notes in pencil, but I fear
they are chancy at the best. I came down in a motor with

Valentine*, who is sort of general supervisor of the aircraft Park, that's the base, he buys spares etc. He has a very nice motor provided for him and we came down in great comfort. Paris is very different from when we came through, it's quite like ordinary now. Well I must be off to Buc so best of love to you dearest mother.
DENYS

*NOTE: Valentine was a bumptious character who had learned to fly with CW at Pau.

Farm House, France. 1st November, 1914

Dearest Mother,

Just in from reconnaissance over German lines. A most lovely day, climbed to 7,200 feet and my observer saw splendidly, we went a good round and he poked out a battery which they've been wanting to know about, also saw large quantities of horses and motor lorries at their rail head, or what we take to be their rail head.

I had a very nice trip here from Paris, the machine seems a very good one. I think I told you the other was scrapped as unsafe. I'm on duty tonight so am sleeping down in our small camp by the machines.

We are billeted here in a farmhouse, but one officer has to sleep with the machines.

The guns have knocked off for a bit and it's only an occasional one now – at 5.45pm. Today nothing worried us at all at that height, but if at all low they bother us quite a bit. A German machine came over this morning and our fellows here started firing at it. However it was miles out of range, but the staff at H.Q. thought that the Germans had got round and were making an attack in the rear!

Half a squadron of Native Cavalry came galloping up to know what it was, – such fine fellows*. Their officer stopped and had a yarn with us. Bengal Cavalry. They had hardly ever seen an aeroplane before. I hear that news is distinctly good. All round a certain town we passed over today the ground was literally ploughed up by shell fire, an extraordinary sight. There is still desultory artillery fire going on, one just pooped off and another, so I suppose they'll rumble on all night. It was a lovely night but big dark clouds are coming up. I fear it may rain before long. I'm lying on straw with two old Bleriot wings propped up to make a tent. Quite snug and comfy, with one of the motor transport oil side lamps for light. One night here I lay awake listening to a very devil of a night scrap. Musketry, machine guns, the whole business, it didn't last long, but it was "werry sharp". I did admire the Indian Cavalry; they do sit well on their horses, beautiful horsemen I thought them, and well mounted. A high explosive, – one of the big guns, has just 'pooped off' – he makes a horrid noise, some of our people go out each day observing for batteries, telling them by means of lights how their shots are going. I haven't done that. I think it sounds a very difficult job. On reconnaissance we go out over a country agreed on beforehand, and I just dodge about as my observer wants me to. He enjoyed his flight today; it was so clear, and he got on to some good things. At H.Q. where we were last week, our anti-aircraft gun fired 21 shots at a Taube [Dove] not much good, he was very high and a long way off. It's funny to see shrapnel bursting, sometimes, you think they are near the machine when they're probably a long way away really. One of our people on a fast single seater started off in pursuit of a Taube some days ago, but though he saw him clouds were low and he lost him in one.

I'm very well and fit. I saw Marcelle in Paris; she sent you her love. She's off to Egypt. I'm glad you have a nice flat. Thanks for the parcel.

Guns quiet again, a great many burning villages, today all over the place. Moon's out again now, it's a lovely night.

So glad Heydeman got decorated. [He was from the English family of German origin.] The Bays have done splendidly I believe.

Two heavy guns again. There has been very heavy fighting on our extreme left. The Germans have been doing their utmost to get through to Calais, but I hear all goes well and we are advancing slowly. My servant has just come down with my blankets and made all snug. Someone will come down and relieve me while I get a bit of dinner – any time now.

I brought lots of papers back from Paris which were much appreciated, also a pate and some under-clothing.

I wish you'd send me out a revolver, not too heavy, to take the ordinary Government No. 450 ammunition, which I can get out here.

There's a high road just near, about 200 yds off, and hundreds of transport motor wagons, ambulance, and all sorts pass through most of the day and night, – and always lots of refugees. If we can only hang on, as we are doing a bit longer, I think they'll go back pretty soon. One hears they are getting more than they like. It's a terrible mix-up, Turkey going to war now. I can hear two of the men arguing as to the position of Jack Johnson**. It sounds so funny. J.J. is one of the German big howitzers, there are J.J.'s, Black Marias and Archibald's.

Well, I must go up and get some dinner.
    Best of love to you, dearest Mother,
    Ever your loving, D

*NOTE: In some of his letters, CW commented on the fortitude and bearing of the Indian troops. At the outbreak of war, the Indian Army immediately offered two infantry and two cavalry divisions for service anywhere. This force was originally destined for Egypt to relieve British troops there, but at the last minute was diverted to France where the divisions were thrown into the Battle of La Bassée in October/November 1914. The Indian troops showed remarkable courage, though all suffered from the cold and from homesickness, and indeed from unfamiliar equipment, some regiments having only just received Lee-Enfield rifles.

**NOTE: Jack Johnson was a black man who was contemporary heavyweight champion of the world; his victories provoked racist reaction in the United States. Archibald, or 'Archie', was the name given by British fliers when dodging enemy anti-aircraft bursts; they sang the popular music hall ditty: 'Archibald, certainly not!'

4th November, 1914

Dearest Mother,

Such a lovely day. Did three reconnaissance, but we saw little movement, they lie very dogo now when they see us coming. We cruised about trying to get a 4.7 battery on their target. We got them on in the morning, but spent a useless hour in the afternoon waiting for their shots, cruising over the battery they were trying to hit. After a bit we went back to see why they didn't fire as agreed, and my observer in going over after landing found them moving their guns, as it meant that or cutting down a lot of trees. They had been firing wide and when we got there they found they had to move and get their range. However it's all very interesting. Germans made no effort to shell us, but we got some rifle fire very slight. I think they are moving N. concentrating their things. We're quietish today here. My observer today was a Captain in the Black Watch Staff College Special Observer. We had a most sumptuous lunch with a detachment of this regiment, but most of their

Officers were in the trenches so we didn't see them. The Indian contingent are all round here, they have suffered a good deal, I fear. The Germans have made their effort here, and I think they must be moving North to try again to get through to the Coast and Calais. My new machine I brought from Paris so far has proved really good, it climbs well, and is a very nice flyer, quite unlike that other old box. One of our special observers here is a very keen fox hunter and we have many a yarn together over the chase. I wonder if they are hunting in Kilkenny. It's hard to get news here but things seem good. Certainly the shelling is less tonight.

Hope tomorrow will be fine again, today was a joy. Best of love to you, dearest Mother, hope the flat's a success.

DENYS

Man wrote about Jock, [still in quarantine] asking for him to be removed as he was over-crowded. Do go and see after him.

CHAPTER TWELVE

Forward Base

Corbett Wilson had barely a fortnight to get accustomed to his new home when the autumn gales set in – sometimes these were strong enough to force an aircraft to fly backwards! November was wet as well as windy when No. 3 Squadron moved to a new aerodrome at Choques, whose landing strip had been a beet field with a very uneven surface. Luckily, a nearby Indian cavalry unit had a roller, which was borrowed to help with the levelling process, but still the boots of every available man in the squadron were needed and the unit marched and counter-marched to press down the beet roots. Even after all this treatment the ground was still soft and just about good enough for a landing, so the CO ordered quantities of cinders from a nearby gasworks, which improved matters.

Hangars were erected but gales would spring up to blow them down again, while the rain poured in torrents. In an attempt at drainage, deep ditches were dug around the hangars and every so often a loud splash, accompanied by curses would announce that another unfortunate mechanic had fallen in. Despite the awful conditions, artillery reconnaissance was continuously undertaken: the crew of one Bleriot averaged six-and-half hours in the air each day for a week. Conditions changed and by the middle of November there was a heavy fall of snow and the weather became intensely cold. Chores such as changing the engine of a Bleriot in the open with frozen fingers were difficult: paradoxically some mechanics would sleep at night under the wings of their charges.

C Flight, to which CW was attached, remained at this forward field but the flight soon followed the squadron to St. Omer. Here, there were rumours that the Bleriots would shortly be replaced with Moranes, but this did not happen until the end of the year.

CHAPTER THIRTEEN

Letters:
5 to 24 November 1914

5th November, 1914.

Dearest Mother,

Just back to H.Q. to find your letter and parcel. Thanks for things. Everything is most acceptable, but I've plenty of warm things now, and am never cold. Was over 5 hours in the air today. I wonder if you get my letters?

The machine I brought from Paris has gone well, and is a very nice machine to fly. You see I'm writing with your block you sent, most successful affair. It's hard to give you news: we know so little. I think things are much the same, no advance and no retirement 'non plus' [either]. Today after our reconnaissance I went up to the big 60 pounder battery to try and get them on to their target. We got them on to two, but it's slow work. They got one hit plum on the factory held by the Germans, the infantry had sent special word that they wanted this particular factory shelled. The old chap in command [of the artillery battery] is not over quick and misses his direction half the time; it's rather maddening. I always feel it's a waste of an aeroplane and two men's time, but it is not really, as if you can get them on once they can go on shelling till there's nothing left and so our infantry can advance. Still as I say it's a slow and rather irritating job, especially when they don't fire in answer to us when we signal ready.

It's been a lovely day. I landed just at dark. We have a most comfy billet, quite a chateau. It rained in torrent last night. I was sorry for the people in the trenches. We were on our farm then and three of us motored into the nearest town and went to the Etablissement des Bains, and had a real hot bath apiece, – very nice indeed, and quite clean.

Well, I'm very weary, so goo-night [a memory of childhood]. Much love.
D.

NOTE: The following three letters were written on the same day.

6th November, 1914.

Dearest Mother,

We've been having desperate weather, but today was fine. I did some artillery work with a man named Powell who is ordinarily a master at Eton I believe! Tomorrow I shall do some more with an Engineer Captain observer. It's rather dull work as so often they [Allied artillery] don't fire, either from not seeing the signals properly or for some reason of their own. However, we always do a short reconnaissance first to see our target.

My machine has been going well, may it continue. Now the bad weather has come they don't like the Bleriots to go far away from home, as with these strong winds they think they might never get back.

A parcel from F & M [Fortnum & Mason] arrived with very good things in it. Will you send in the next one potted meats and a pate if possible, also a cold plum pudding. Cholmondely brought one back from Paris yesterday. I lunched at their mess today and ate quite well as much as was good for me. I'm also rather getting low in cigarettes, will you send some more from the same place, Freiburg & Treyer. My plans [for bombing Berlin] are maturing but there are difficulties. Trenchard, however, recommended it, but I fear it has to go for approval to several other ossiffers [sic] of exalted ranks. Ca marche [all's well] in Russia. The cartoons in Punch have been so good, haven't they lately?

Much love to you, I'm very fit and well so far. Thick pants arrived, splendid ones.
DENYS

NOTE: The prevailing winds over the Western Front were Westerly which represented a headwind for the Allied airmen, making return flights to base very difficult on occasion, while favouring the German aviators returning home. The sun as well was more beneficial to the German airmen.

I find I shall have after all to go on here as I seem to have exhausted space over leaf. We went right through the Indian Corps lines today, when visiting the battery I was observing for, and met dozens of these funny mule carts they drive, they are a most dignified looking people. We often have them out here, patrolling etc, the other day it was the Jodphur Lancers mounted on wiry little rats of ponies all with good limbs and bones. I believe they are the Rajah's own private troops. We are very snug in the cottage. Will you send out some of the Xmas numbers of Illustrated Papers, Tatler etc and magazines. I've already ended the letter once and now dinner is ready so must stop. I don't know Cristelles [sic] address I haven't seen Carpenter since.

Love to you again dearest mother,
D.

We reported 2 long artillery trains going N.E., looks as if they are moving off, only leaving sufficient to hold on here. I hear we could advance, but don't owing to disease in German lines at Lille.

We've got an ammunitions train, the Indian Corps billeted over the way here, all the Indians sitting round their fires near their horse lines.

No news in the front, they still hold La Bassee, it looks like deadlock for the winter.

Billet, N. France
9th November, 1914

Dearest Mother,

Glad to hear you got two letters, but you ought to have had more than that. I fear several must have not got through. I've given one or two to be posted to different people, and I suppose they've probably lost them; however, I don't think they could have been censored, as I've not given away any news, – and I don't know any! I lent my writing block to a sportsman who has not yet returned it. I've unearthed this in our billet which is quite comfy, country house, semi Chateau, the people have cleared out, I believe the owner is himself at the "Guerre". The last few days have been hopeless from reconnaissance point of view. Very foggy and today is worse. Clouds are only about 300 feet up.

The camp is damp and unpleasant, still we've had splendid weather till now and yesterday was sunny though too misty to be any use for observing. We get very conflicting reports, and one never gets anything much to believe. "On dit" [they say] that the news is good, and I really can't help thinking that if the Germans fail this time to get through they'll be in a very bad way, both as regards morale and losses. Our people have been losing terribly too, the casualty lists are fearsome, but we don't lose ground, as far as we can hear. There was a big battle going on last night away to the North. We could hear the heavy guns for hours. No one has done a reconnaissance for four days now, owing to the fog. Hope to get news soon as I feel sure this time is most critical. To read the Daily Mail and such-like one would think that Germany is in a very bad way and that we are fighting a nation of barbarians. How far this is true I don't know, but I hear a great deal of this atrocity business is much exaggerated, and that for the most part they behave well. I don't know whether I told you that the last time I was piloting an artillery observer, the Major in charge of the battery we were observing for, had been specially asked by our infantry to shell a certain factory and surrounding houses held by the Germans. Well, it appears we got them on to it well, and the infantry sent back special thanks in consequence. I know one shot landed in the courtyard or garden. I expect it was that one that put them out – they were big 60 pounders, and one or two of these well placed cause some damage.

I'm sorry for the Indians this cold, damp weather. I saw quite a lot of them one day.

Is it Washington House, Basil Street? I shall send them to 3 Hans.

Chocolate you sent is much appreciated.

Best love to you, Dearest Mother, do rescue old Jock. I enclose another letter from Whitehall, but it doesn't affect him, as far as I can see, expect that the time is now reduced to 4 months, so you might get two off this, and then he would be nearly ready for release now.
DENYS.

Today a gardener has turned up here and is planting bulbs in the garden, this looks as if the inhabitants were getting confidence once again.

November 11th, 1914

[NOTE: CW was promoted to Lieutenant on this day. The war would last four more long years before the Armistice was signed also on this date].

You needn't put "Aeronautic" on my letters, that's only the telegraphic address.

Dearest Mother,

It's blowing a gale of wind. I'm waiting in a tent which inadequately shelters my Bleriot and another. While I was at lunch they've had to take the wings off both for safety. I think the tent may go at any moment!!

We've just been out round the tent pegs, some of which were looking like departing. If it freshens any more I am sure the whole show will go. We are in a very exposed position highish up, and we get all there is of it. We've hardly done anything lately, the weather has been vile.

Yesterday was a blank day for me. I was on 'Taube chasing' which means if any hostile aircraft, as they call them, come over, it is your particular duty to either chase them off or do them in. Today I was first for reconnaissance, but we couldn't start, clouds at 200 ft, thick, and a gale towards German lines, so that we should have gone down wind like blazes, but would never have got back, also incidentally making a fine target of ourselves for all the German 'Archibalds' – all along the line. It's disappointing weather this from our point of view as when we are not actually flying, we do nothing – there is nothing to do. Of course there is one's machine, you can always fuss round, but when one gets 5 or 6 days of it (bad weather) it gets very tiresome.

'They' say that it blows like this all winter, so encouraging. This old tent is flapping something outrageous. There is a poor old Henri Farman outside, tied to earth by every device of man. I'm not sure it is not better off than in this flapping tent. Of course it is of the oldest and rottenest. Why if they have tents at all they can't have newish ones I cannot imagine. They take the trouble of carting this ancient relic of another age about where a new one would take no more room and do its job better. Most of the machines are out in the open, so we must be thankful our Bleriots are in somewhere. The fact is the Bleriots won't stand being out long, they run very quickly to seed.

News seems apparently not much changed, seems encouraging though. We advance slowly. No more paper. Best love,
D.

We have a captured German machine here; it's a copy of the Morane almost entirely.

———————————

North France
12th November, 1914

Dearest Mother,

I forgot yesterday to tell you to put No. 3 Squadron, RFC, Expeditionary Force, France, on my letters and parcels. there is another Wilson and it causes confusion. I've not yet had the parcel from Wilkinson, – perhaps he has it! He is not here, and sometimes I get his letters. Last night all the tents blew down! However, no apparent damage is done, but chaos reigned this morning. It's a pity the new machines got hardship so early, both my Bleriot and [that of] Pretyman's were nearly new. Still the wings don't look any the worse. It's blowing hard and very low clouds.

I believe Lord Roberts came up to the ground yesterday, but it was such a vile day no one saw him. He's a wonderful old chap. It's dull doing no flying, but it's just useless at present. We hear today the 1st Corps has done very well yesterday and slain many Germans. The worst of the job is that we are helpless when the weather is like this, one cannot do any reconnaissance with low clouds and a high wind, at least not with this wind which sets towards the German lines.

I'm getting my wings put on again today preparatory to having the machine in a better shed. It was extraordinary that our two Bleriots weren't destroyed last night. I was in bed when a bedraggled officer came in last night to say all the tents were down. As I was first for reconnaissance he thought he'd come in and let me know I need not get up early, owing to the general chaos, wings off, everything strewn about, – anyway the weather would not permit.

Hope the flat's a success.

Much love to you, dear Mother, D.

NOTE: Lord Roberts, much loved, and known as "Bobs" by his troops, had been the British Commander-in-Chief in the Boer War.

St Omer
15th November, 1914

Dearest Mother,

One of our people is going home, this by him.

Will you send me that green folding mattress that I discarded from my valise, very foolish. I want it when I go out on detachment. It should have been with my things at Brooklands. If it is not will you get another at Wilkinson's, he will know; it is part of the Valise equipment.

Yesterday I did a small job, had to go out to our detached post near Bethune, from where I wrote to you first from the farm house, to pick up observer for reconnaissance, as one of their pilot's engines was out of order, and he was changing it. 'A' Flight are out there now, they relieved us. Bethune was being shelled by the Germans. Clouds were low, and day did not improve. However, we packed off and did a short reconnaissance over La Bassee. Bois de Biez, up their [German] line nearly to Armentieres. Then as my man said we weren't doing much good; he couldn't pick up much owing to clouds, we landed at Estaires for artillery observation for a 60 pounder. But it was a poor day which did not improve till late. Took 50 minutes to do 20 miles coming home, and that very low. At three thousand I was standing still. Our usual round from here for reconnaissance is Menin, Coutrai, Lille, Roubaix, Tourcoing, Auber, La Bassee.

This man [the courier going on leave] is just off so must stop. Got pistol – thanks.

Get old Jock out. There is a battle going on today at Messines.

Much love to you, dearest Mother,
Ever your loving,
D.

———————————

November 16th, 1914.

Dearest Mother,

I am sleeping in camp tonight, on duty, my house is one of the motor lorries on the edge of the aviation ground. I sent a scrawl to you yesterday by one of our people who was going home, but I was very rushed as he was just off. The weather is vile, as I told you in that letter I did a short reconnaissance day before yesterday and some artillery observation but it was a bad day and my observer had in the end to give up. The names of all the places are now given in the papers so I don't see why I shouldn't tell you where we go. Our usual round from here at Omer [RFC headquarters] is Menin, Coutrai, Roubaix, Tourcoing, Lille, Tonmar, Auber, La Bassee. I was sent out to our landing ground near Bethune which was being shelled, to do this job of one of A Flight's pilots whose motor was being repaired. I landed at Hinges to pick up the necessary observer and we then pushed off to try and locate some new batteries north of La Bassee near the famous Bois de Biez – where so much hard fighting has been going on. We passed over the Bois and though we were mostly in cloud he managed to pick up one of the batteries by the flashes.

Corbett Wilson wearing his favourite flying jacket, purchased at Pau where he learnt to fly. CW is about to start the journey, which culminated in the first flight across the Irish Sea.

Darver House, near Kilkenny City, a substantial residence leased by the Corbett Wilsons.

Left: Edwardian elegance. The Corbett Wilsons could afford the lifestyle of these well-heeled Edwardians. The chauffeur of the Rolls Royce is dimly seen in the background – he knows his place!

Right: CW pictured with his faithful companion "Jobbles Jock" about whom he fretted while the animal was quarantined in Britain when the family returned from Italy in 1914.

Following the Kilkenny hunt: CW mounted on his favourite horse. Both he and his mount survived a couple of hunting accidents.

Hendon Aerodrome circa 1911. Thousands made the journey to north London to enjoy the air race competitions and displays.

CW's mechanic is about to swing the propeller to start a flight.

Aerial view of the Bleriot School at Pau during CW's training there. (*Courtesy Musée de l'air et de l'Espace, Paris*)

Hangers at Pau. Similar hangarage was available at the other Bleriot School near Paris. (*Courtesy Musée de l'air et de l'Espace, Paris*)

New Edwardian hobby: in the early 1900s the wealthy could indulge in the new art of flying. Here Vivian Hewitt, who would later become a rival of Corbett Wilson, is flying over the sands of Rhyl in his native Wales.

Landing at Crane, Co. Wexford: CW's Bleriot was not equipped with wheel brakes (a refinement sometimes missing on aircraft right up to the 1930s), hence it ran on until "arrested" by a gorse bank. The aviator's signature and the date is just discernible at the bottom ot the photograph.

CW returns to Crane prior to flying his machine to the polo grounds.

Top: Near Colva, high in the Welsh mountains, on April 20th 1912: the Bleriot is ready for its final leg southwards to its jumping-off point near Fishguard.

Centre: With its engine protected by bushes and its rudder also covered, CW's Bleriot is admired by a crowd at the polo grounds. All are looking forward to another dramatic flight by their hero!

Bottom: All set for take-off: CW's mechanic gives a final check over the Bleriot.

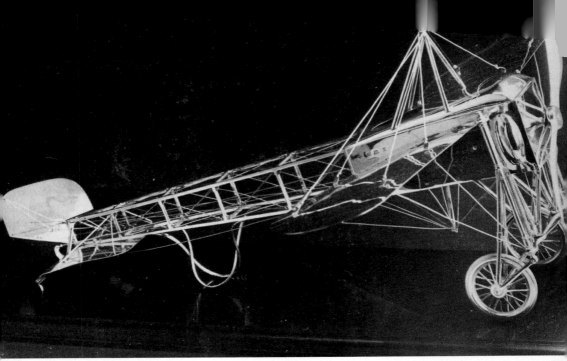

The detailed silver model of CW's Bleriot presented to him by the ctizens of Kilkenny to mark his extraordinary feats in the air. For a while this model was displayed in the nascent Irish Aviation Museum at Dublin Airport.

CW shows the strain of a rough flight on landing at Powerstown Park Racecourse prior to giving a display there. Stewards hold back the large crowd.

Monsieur Vial, CW's second mechanic, is engaged in an overhaul of the Bleriot at its base at Kilkenny polo grounds.

An unsupervised naughty Irish boy tests an elevator with his boot! Many adults too were unaware of the flimsy nature of the new-fangled aeroplanes.

As he had promised after his disaster at Clonmel, CW returns to give a splendid display.

Mrs Corbett Wilson, escorted by an ex-naval officer, is viewing her son's display at Waterford in 1913 with a mixture of interest and apprehension.

Mrs Corbett Wilson and a policeman gaze on the wrecked Bleriot following the bad landing at the racecourse. The wrecked aircraft was shipped back to the Bleriot factory near Paris for a complete rebuild.

Corbett Wilson bought this two-seater 80hp Bleriot which enabled him to make some of his friends air-minded, if not perhaps air-sick!

CW returns to Clonmel to give the display which had earlier been cancelled due to a crash landing.

The military version of the Bleriot XI-2 which No. 3 Squadron used in the early days of the war.

August 1914. No. 3 Squadron has arrived at Amiens which would have been the site of the Aircraft Park, but the rapid German advance caused it to be re-sited at St. Omer. (*Courtesy RAF Museum*)

A British 9.2 inch howitzer, nicknamed "Mother" goes into action. This ponderous weapon, developed on the eve of the Great War, had to be laboriously dismantled into three loads for transportation behind either horse teams or tractors, and then put together at their firing sites. (*Courtesy Imperial War Museum*)

This German howitzer is typical of the quarry which CW and his RFC comrades were continually seeking to pinpoint so that Allied artillery could eliminate them.

The British Prime Minister, David Lloyd George, on a visit to the Western Front, converses with two Indian officers. The Indian troops were much admired by CW.

CW admired the French Colonial Spahi cavalry. Here a guard-of-honour is saluting a visiting dignitary with sabres raised. (*Courtesy Imperial War Museum*)

Dramatic study of Morane No. 3260 of No. 3 Squadron being run up before take off.

Here is an example of some of the landing grounds which the RFC had to operate from. On the waterlogged surface of a No. 3 Squadron aerodrome, an early Morane is visible together with some war-weary Bleriots.

Captain E. L. Conran beside his Morane. The prominent windscreen protects the observer in this otherwise primitive machine – which is probably the one passed on to CW when repaired after Conran's serious combat injuries.

Below: The captured German aircraft which CW refers to in his letter. Its wings have been removed and it is being guarded on No. 3 Squadron's airfield by some French poilus. (*Courtesy RAF Museum*)

The British 60-pounder, seen on the left, is about to go into action when the advancing field battery has cleared its position. Despite its deceptively slender looks, this medium gun weighed $5^1/2$ tons and was used in both World Wars.

The German firm of Krupp was instrumental in developing a 75mm high angle weapon for use against airships and aircraft. The prototype was tried out in the summer manoeuvres of 1909 and became the first really effective mobile anti-aircraft weapon. It is highly likely that it was this type of gun which brought down Corbett Wilson and his observer Woodiwiss in May 1915. (*Both photographs courtesy The Imperial War Museum*)

A Morane Type L of No. 3 Squadron takes off. Its developed version, known as the Type LA, incorporated many refinements.

2nd Lt. Newton Woodiwiss stands in front of a wrecked aircraft from which he escaped just a few days before he was shot down with CW in May 1915. (*Courtesy 'Aeroplane'*

Sgt. James McCudden, who would later become Major J.T.B. McCudden, V.C., D.S.O., *, M.M., Croix de Guerre With 57 victories to his credit he was the fourth most successful fighter pilot on the Alllied side.

Left: During the hectic retreat from Mons, R.F.C. personnel grab a quick bite to eat. (*Courtesy the RAF Museum*)

Above: A Morane Type L which was delivered direct from Paris to No. 3 Squadron on 22nd March, 1915 and was returned to the Aircraft Park on 25th September of that year. (*Courtesy the RAF Museum*)

Below: Sgt. Frank Courtney of No. 3 Squadron stands in front of his Morane Type L which has a tail fin fitted. After the war, Courtney was a well-known figure in American and European aviation. (*Courtesy the RAF Museum*)

Shortly after Corbett Wilson's demise in a Morane Type L, No. 3 Squadron was fully equipped with the type LA.

Damer Leslie Allen sits in the cockpit of his Bleriot XI.

Last minute advice for D.L. Allen before he takes off from Hendon on his flight to Ireland.

They generally cease firing when we come over, but I suppose they thought we shouldn't see them on such a day, clouds were so low. We then landed at Estaires, for Artillery observation, as observer could not make much of a reconnaissance. We drove from the landing ground to the Battery, a 60 pounder – by motor, to find out what particular target the Battery Commander wants to be got on to. On the way, you could see the effect of the German shell-fire; in one field there were 5 holes quite close to a house. I suppose the 6th knocked it down – all 5 very close together, very accurate shooting, artillery plays a big part but it's the infantry that wins the day. I got a nice old shaking up coming home, wind had got up, took 5 minutes to do 20 miles [24mph!]. It's raining and I fear this old lorry is going to leak, felt a drop then!

Today was another hopeless day of storms and wind. I took up a passenger this afternoon, on a bomb dropping experiment to test a new bomb, a nice old shaking we got too. Wind high and gusty, – neither of the precious bombs exploded. Something wrong with the ignition [detonator] business – we must try again tomorrow. Lots of majors and people out to see the effect of these wondrous bombs – some disappointment – the man next for reconnaissance went out this morning but had to come back owing to storms before he's got 20 miles – it's very disappointing, this weather.

Got the pistol – it's quite all right. It will do fine.

I want you to send me out my green rolling mattress that was with my valise and which I foolishly discarded – it should have been with my things at Brooklands, I want it for when we are on detachment at a farm house. My dinner has just come – so here goes – soup, curry, cheese – not so bad and very good cocoa.

Message just come through saying the detachment at Bethune is in difficulty for two machines tomorrow, so I expect I shall have to go in another. I've sent the message on to the major. All the orderlies have motor bicycles, they are most useful in war. The wireless news today wasn't much. I can't make out whether Dixmude is ours or not. All attacks repulsed. Expect we shall be going out on detachment again soon almost every other week, but the weather had been so bad that they have not been doing anything and so need no rest and will carry on a bit longer I expect. Yes. Do go and get the old dog out. I'm sure he's not comfy there. Never got Wilkinson's parcel yet.

So Baldoo is not to be married – thought it seemed funny.

Well good night dearest Mother, Your loving, D.

If you can't find mattress will you get another at Wilkinson's.

So sad poor old Lord Roberts dying here – it was given out at Church parade.

19th November, 1914

Dearest Mother,

Wilkinson's parcel has arrived at last, such nice socks, and the blanket is very acceptable, also the cigarettes. I shan't want socks for a bit, I am giving what I don't want away. Chocolates arrived and still more socks today.

It's now snowing hard and very cold. Nothing doing today, but yesterday did a reconnaissance over Lille and surrounding country. There was a most 'orrible drift on, and we took an awful time to get to Armentieres. Then I gave it up and drifted away over Lille, to do that side. I wanted to get away up to Menin, and around that side, but we were taking too long, we should never have got there. Coming home I had to steer due North to get West. [An example of 'drift'] Coming here, however, we saw lots of German transport trains and batteries. My observer was out for his first time, and was very taken up with the shell bursting business.

Today has been quite impossible, and now there is three or four inches of snow, and very cold indeed.

Two French biplanes have arrived on their way to Dunkerque. One won't start, and the other I do not know what is wrong. They are Voisins machines much used by the French.

One hears that if the Germans don't get through tonight, they mean to retire – but we have had some of that story before, and nothing happened – nothing new anyway.

I expect we are in for a hard winter. It's funny to see such snow in November.

Colonel Trenchard has turned up here. I believe he is to have command of Nos. 2 and 3 Squadrons, hope he does, he is a good man, and good men are rather wanted.

Saw Carpenter in the town yesterday, he said he had a poor job, looking after bridges or something. Said Cristel was in London. He was very cheery and I asked him to come here for a meal. He's billeted some way out.

Much love to you.
D

Aviation Ground, 6.30pm
24th November, 1914

Dearest Mother,

Had a rattling day today, over five hours in the air. Poor Loraine, my observer, was slightly, I hope, wounded. We got him to Hospital as quickly as possible and he's quite comfy now though in some pain. Of course we had to give it up when he was hit, but the reconnaissance was important, the French thought they were going to try a very strong attack from La Bassee way, and information was much wanted as regards movements of troops on the railway. The wind was so strong we couldn't get against it, but had to sidle up the position as far as Armentieres and then drift across keeping her head to wind more or less.

We saw very little movement really on the line, all clear as far as Warvin, but I should not be surprised if they are thinking of attacking again there, as we were very much fired at. This was the last reconnaissance for the day, and there was a delay at the start owing to my right-hand shock absorber [made up of twisted rubber strands] having perished in the frost. It had stretched and let the machine down on one side so had to be replaced at the last moment, and as we had so little time before dark, we hadn't time to climb more than 5,000 feet, still I hope he's not too bad. I got him home very quickly down wind, 5,000 is usually fairly safe, but standing against the wind made it easier for them to make some good shooting. Today, it was a job to get him out of the machine, he kept saying all the time we were getting him out "all clear as far as Warvin".

He is the actor Robert Loraine, the once flying man now turned observer [see next chapter for his attainments pre-war]. He joined the Corps at the beginning of the war and has been doing good work, I believe, observing. It's one thing the RFC never took into consideration, the observer question. Consequently they are very short of good men to observe. Loraine has taken great trouble and studied it up, and is very keen. [This was a strange development. Loraine had been re-mustered from pilot because of eyesight trouble – yet now he was an observer!]

We have had frost and snow, lovely days, but very cold and high N.E. wind at anything over 2,000 feet. I've any amount of warm things though, and today was as warm as toast all day, feet and all – quite a triumph. I wear galoshes over my ordinary boots with great success, also leather trousers and really I was warmer in the machine than out. The machine has been going very well, may it continue. What's wrong with uncle Julian? I never gathered that: give him my love; yes, I fear Yawl was a bit of a ruffian. Glad you like the flat. The Germans don't make any headway, still they don't go back. I fear it's going to be some tussle.

I find I've written all over this now, so must start another. Yes, I should like some Fortnum & Mason stuff, it would be much appreciated by No. 3 Squadron mess. Thanks for the mattress, arrived safe. I left my other with my kit at Brooklands, but the one you sent is a most superior one.

I thought I saw a German machine today in the distance, but on pursuing found it was one of our traction biplanes [probably a Vickers Gun Bus]. They have a strong resemblance to the German. They got a German yesterday and one today, the first landed in our lines owing to motor trouble, and the other was brought down by some of our people's guns, I believe. I believe one is undamaged and is to come here, it will be interesting to see it. Poor old Jock, I hope he's happy.

Well goo [sic] night, dearest mother. Much love to you. D.

CHAPTER FOURTEEN

Lt-Col Robert Loraine, RFC

Robert Loraine, a notable actor who had played the lead in many of George Bernard Shaw's dramas, was a keen balloonist in the early days of the twentieth century; he had in fact taken the dramatist for his first aerial trip. But the success of the Wright brothers with heavier-than-air craft caused him to forsake ballooning and take to the air in a Henry Farman biplane. On 10 August 1910 he had established an over-sea world record by covering 60 miles until lack of fuel caused him to land at the northern end of Anglesey. He was keen to be the first across the Irish Sea and he continued from Holyhead. His target was the large expanse of the Phoenix Park in Dublin.

Initially, he climbed to 4000 feet before it became evident that, after a previous minor landing incident, his aircraft had not been properly re-rigged. He began to hear the ominous 'ping, ping' of flying wires snapping – the Farman had a large web of structural wires. As if that was not enough, the machine's Gnome rotary engine stopped dead, but when he dived to 500 feet, it came alive again. This performance was repeated five times before he sighted the Irish coast, north of Dublin.

Loraine continued to climb and then dive because it was now obvious to him that his engine problem was due to fuel starvation and this method would give temporary relief. But every dive caused more flying wires to snap! He actually crossed the coastline but fearing that the whole machine would fold up in the air, he went about half-a-mile out to sea and came down. He now had to swim for his life, but luckily a packet steamer picked him up. Ironically, the play in which he had been appearing in London was entitled 'The Man from the Sea'.

Robert Loraine could have claimed that he was the first to fly across the Irish Sea, but he never did so. 'Bob' Loraine continued to fly and was an early member of the RFC and was soon posted to No. 3 Squadron. On the day he was flying with CW they were again on Artillery Fire Control. There was a very strong easterly head wind, which practically brought them to a standstill over the German AA (anti-aircraft) guns. Loraine, with theatrical bravado, dropped a note to the Germans: 'Keep your eye in, we will be back this afternoon!' True to their word, they were back and spent three-quarters-of-an-hour directing artillery fire while their engine was at full throttle, beating into the persistent east wind. Then a bullet from a shrapnel shell hit Loraine in the back and crossed his right lung from top to bottom, coming out just under the collarbone in front. He later wrote in his diary, with all the panache of an actor:

> As my reconnaissance was of immediate importance, I tried to continue, but found that details were utterly beyond me. So I asked Corbett Wilson to go back to our landing ground, telling him I was hit. Then, as there was nothing else to do, I fainted.

In hospital it was touch and go for a time, but Loraine recovered and served on to the end of the war by which time he was a Lt-Col with a bar to his DSO. Afterwards, he continued his successful theatrical career.

CHAPTER FIFTEEN

Letters: 25 November to 25 December 1914

25th November, 1914

Dearest Mother,

Just got yours with list of food! Yes, most certainly they would be acceptable if you could manage to get one of F. & M.'s Strasburg pies (pate de fois gras) you'll have to pay £1 for it, also a good plum cake, but I see that's mentioned. Cakes, rich plum ones, are much appreciated!! Also would half a Stilton be too heavy? We are a good many and would soon have it down; it would not have any time to go bad on us.

I wrote you some time ago saying I had got Wilkinson's parcel of socks and blankets, very nice indeed.

Things seem about the same. If you get hold or hear of any good novels, will you send them? We've got the long evening nowadays. Papers illustrated etc., like you send are very welcome, specially Tatler, Sketch, Punch, Bystander.

We've another German machine here now, such a heavy looking thing, but I should think good, and very comfortable. It's got 120 hp Mercedes engine in it. Two youths were flying it and got brought down near Hinges. No, we don't need any butter; we get quite good ration butter, and the meat is generally very good indeed. The socks you sent were splendid. Will you send me two pairs soft thickish drawers (long ones).

We are still in our comfy billet here in St Omer, compared to the people trembling in the trenches we are indeed lucky, and well off. I believe also now the Major has found a most comfy Chateau for our billet near Bethune, for our detachment job, so we ought to be comfy over there. The farmhouse was pretty primitive.

I hope you get all my letters. Wrote you a long letter the other evening, dated it 25th outside, but it was only the 23rd really. We never know the day of the week or the date. Nothing to tell you since that the frost has gone leaving fogs and dampness. I've not been out since two days, and now even am not next for reconnaissance as we've not been able to do any. My wounded observer, Loraine, goes on well, they tell me, or rather as well as can be expected. I can't get to see him, as he's in hospital at Bethune, but when we got out there again, on detachment, shall go and see after him. No news.

Much love to you, dear Mother.
D.

25th November 1914

I find I can't enclose all this, must find an envelope to put the whole bag of tricks in. I do hope that old dog gets exercise, – vous croyez? [what do you think?].

Tea has just arrived, the curtains are drawn, lamp lit,

fire going, people toasting bread; if you picture us
campaigning, we ain't.

No more news,
Love again,
D.

November 29th, 1914

Dearest Mother,

We've moved out again from St. Omer and now the whole
squadron is out at an old place near Bethune only they've
changed the landing ground to make room for all of us. A
and B flights are billeted in a chateau nearby, but there are
16 of them, awful squeeze, so we have found a cottage
near, empty, and have taken over that, it's quite comfy and
clean with red brick floors. We are on our own and as one
of us says "so much nicer than in that crowd, with all that
hot air". This is an expression much used by these people
meaning "talking shop". Our nice Bleriots are now out in
the open, no sheds, it seems a pity as they deteriorate so
quickly when exposed to weather. We all came here
yesterday in a flock. 5 old ducks headed by the drake on a
single seated machine. Wind over 50 miles an hour. We got
an awful doing as at 1500 feet, though steady we didn't
move and anything under [this altitude], one got tossed
about something dreadful. However, we all got here all
right, I started after Sgt. Cann and got in several minutes
before him, my mechanic who was with me was delighted.
    News there seems none here, things very quite, no guns
now. The Russians seem to be doing well. I went to see
poor Loraine my observer who got hit, yesterday. He is in

hospital at Lillers. He is wonderful well considering and hopes to get off home soon. He was very cheery.

I fear we are in for a slack time, the Bleriots, won't go against strong winds and many days are more or less useless, with the clouds etc. then there are a good number of us I don't think we shall be overworked. We don't know what machines they propose to give us when these Bleriots are done as they will be soon if left out continually. I believe there are some Moranes ordered. I hope so. It's too hopeless going out and standing quite still – the other day we were drifting backwards.

The cakes were much appreciated – rich plum ones, we love.

I can't help wishing something would happen for or against in the war. Standing looking at each other all the winter will be dreadful – and they seem to be rather at an "impasse" now.

Papers illustrated and otherwise are very much appreciated. I wonder if you would have the "Daily Mail" sent to me from their office and ask them if they could make a point of getting it off as early as possible, as a paper of the day before, here is much prized.

The Indian troops are all round here, such fine fellows. Sykes, our colonel, was asking after Peyton, and I said I thought he was either just coming out, or just come out.

What do people in England think of things, how long do they give the war.

Yes, Scott's bill is right, but the compass charged £10 in that other bill should be £5. That was the price but the wretched man wanted £5 for fitting it and he fitted it so badly it was useless, so I declined to pay that, so that bill is right less £5.

I went up to Baileur the other day to try and get to the firing line and see a bit of things but the motor we were in took a skid and ripped the tyres off and delayed us, so we saw nothing except big guns going up and miles of transport. We had a delay at the start too, so altogether it was not a success. Car owner stayed the night and I came back in a wagon lit ambulance train. They were so kind to me. The major in charge of the train saw I got an empty carriage and gave me the "Daily Mail" of the day before. All the wounded seemed most comfy and well cared for. Everyone was most kind. Only about one hour and a half – 20 miles but the train naturally crawls along. We are just going to have lunch, strong smell of cabbage. Your cake is on the table, some eaten.

Best of love to you, dear mother,
D.
Looks like rain

3rd December, 1914

Dearest Mother

I sent you a postcard yesterday, as perhaps letters are not getting through. You don't seem to have got some of mine, as I told you I had the blanket a long time ago. I got your parcel of odds, very useful and much appreciated.

At present we are stuck doing absolutely nothing; it's blowing a gale of wind and heavy storms of rain every few minutes, clouds very low.

I went out yesterday to see some artillery observation, but my observer could not see our target, as a huge bank of cloud came up, just as we had our height and were ready. I took him out over the target to try if he could see through, but he said there was nothing doing, so we came back; it always annoys me, after getting one's height, to be able to do nothing, waste of motor. I fear this kind of weather is pretty prevalent, about now.

I have now got an idea, and have asked permission to try to carry it out; they are supposed to be considering it now; I will let you know full details later if it can come off. [This was probably the resurrection of his plan to bomb Berlin, or a new idea of bombing Essen.]

I fear we shall of necessity be pretty idle this winter, the weather is much against us. I am glad Pietro [their Italian servant at Como] does so well. I always thought him a treasure.

We have bought a large bath, zinc I think, like a big bath shape. Now have fine hot baths, in a sort of spare room of this cottage, which has a fireplace to boil water on. I had one last night and am much benefited.

Much love to you dear Mother.
Yours
D

9th December, 1914

Dearest Mother,

Nothing but fog and rain. We can do nothing. Went up to the firing line this morning to have a look at a landing ground, that we can use if necessary, when working with artillery. There seemed to be a slight scrap going on, some musketry fire and occasional shelling; ground looks quite decent; the trouble is to get a ground not too soft as all the country here is cultivated. Fog is getting worse.

Thanks for paper and books. Will you try and send the papers very up to date as we are <u>so</u> luxurious here that we see quite late papers. Tatler's Xmas No. much appreciated.

Also will you send me some woollen stockings and a pair of gumboots, size 9. I've plenty of stockings in my things at home. I can then wear two pairs of stockings and gum boots and never be wet. At present I wear galoshes over ordinary thick boots but they are wearing out, the galoshes, I mean. These cording boots I brought out are useless, they let in the water. Will you also send my Burberry. I fear we are in for a wet winter.

No move on seems contemplated. I suppose these will be our winter quarters. Poor old machines are sitting solemnly out in it.

Can't you chase them up again about old Jock.

Much love, dear Mother,

Yours

D.

13th December, 1914

Dearest Mother

Absolutely nothing to tell you, fog and rain, quite hopeless for us. They tell us the weather is quite normal and that they expect it all winter. Apparently they don't get much ice and snow, but lots of fog and rain.

I walked up to HQ with Evans this morning, (HQ Indian Corps), but there was no news. The French seem to be progressing a little south of La Bassee, and we reported that they are collecting rolling stock there, perhaps with the idea of a retirement, but what with this enteric plague at Lille and in Belgium I believe a move forward is not particularly wanted yet. It's not much of a prospect for the winter. I fear everyone will be more or less idle except the people actually in the trenches and even they, too, as we hear many Germans have been drawn off. I wish we could advance.

Loraine has gone to England; he was shot through the lungs, poor chap, the bullet went through his British warm coat, also through his leather flying jacket, and was found in his shirt. He'll get all right with care. He was quite cheery when I saw him. It was a shrapnel bullet. [Apart from its casing fragmenting, a shrapnel round dispersed steel balls.]

My plan was to fly to Berlin and try to blow up the Zeppelin sheds there, also to drop pamphlets in Berlin, and through Germany, go on and land amongst the Russians. With this prevailing wind I could have done it, with 8 hours petrol, which with a squeeze I could have got by fitting an auxiliary tank in the passenger's place. Of course, it was a big chance, but Trenchard approved it, but the powers that be say No, not till the spring. Why the spring? When the wind will have gone to the East!

Trenchard is still going at them, however, about it. He rather doubted, too, at first, but I put it to him, from the morale point of view, – seeing a hostile aircraft over their beloved Berlin, etc. I worked myself up to be very keen about it. I really believe it would do an immense amount of good in showing the Germans in Germany that they've got to look out, it should make them think a bit. [This idea presaged General Doolittle's raid on Tokyo with carrier-borne bombers shortly after Pearl Harbor which grievously shocked Japanese morale.] Weight is my chief difficulty, to keep it under maximum for machine, as I must have some petrol in hand, in case I got a contrary wind – 'la bas' [over there] – and petrol weighs heavy when you come to tot it up. Then my bombs also. Still, I could have done it with luck. But Trenchard told me yesterday that 'they' had definitely refused it – till later on.

I must try and work out another for them. A fine lot of good things arrived from F & M, pate de foie gras much appreciated. The smaller fry in tins we are putting by for a rainy day, – as there are several of us, and we get lots of fresh meat so we don't need them yet. The potted meats are always acceptable to do as a savoury or for tea – and cakes. Will you send me some more cigarettes from same place, Freibourg and Treyer? We are living on the fat of the land, everyone has parcels of good things, if I get a chance I'll try and take some tins up to the trenches, as those things like duck and peas etc., would be acceptable [and a welcome change from bully beef and plum jam! CW was always conscious of the atrocious conditions in the trenches]. I've <u>no</u> doubt, but for us fellows who get good fresh meat, well cooked, we don't really need them. I should think tonight will about finish the machines; it's pouring and blowing hard too. I don't think we are enterprising enough in raids, they are not encouraged much, neither is bomb-dropping on military aviation grounds, or the like. I know now pretty well all the aviation grounds in Germany, and was intending taking several on my route; the trouble is you never can get a man like Trenchard – still less the powers that be – down to a map. You see them for a few minutes, and never get a real good yarn with them about the thing. Consequently you forget half the important points. Still I know T recommended it, and I fancy strongly. One can't do more.

Well, good-night, dear Mother. Much love to you,
From D. Those plums you sent from F & M <u>were</u> good.

14th December, 1914
9.30pm

Dearest Mother

Rien de nouveau [nothing new], except that we hope to get
La Bassee tomorrow morning, there is to be a day attack,
they've been shelling the railway triangle two miles west
of La B. where the Germans had some rolling stock also
'les trois maisons' [the three houses]. We tried to help them
[the ground troops] this morning but the clouds persisted
at about 1500 feet – still we did something – I do hope they
get in tomorrow, as La B. seems to have been in great
difficulty, but things seem to be pointing now to an
advance, I only hope it is so.

There is talk of splitting us up for divisional work, but I
don't know if it will come off.

There is a French 75 Battery near one of the 4.7's [sic],
they (the 4.7's [sic]) are wonderfully hidden, in fact the
Battery Commander has moved an entire orchard to hide
his guns, but the 75's [sic] are stuck out in the open for
some extraordinary reason, and so our 4.7's [sic] get some
of the wide German shells aimed at the 75's [sic]; our man
is getting quite 'shirty' about it!

Weather is rotten, windy, cloudy and rainy, my Bleriot
has been out since we left St Omer, in this wretched climate!

Yes, it was funny Walker should have gone to Dr.
Stoker, he hurt his knee [in an accident in CW's aircraft].
My old Bleriot was scrapped as unsafe, still no one realised
how bad it was, it would hardly climb with me alone, let
alone with two and a rifle etc.

Thanks for the papers and parcel, cigarettes chief need
now!

Much love,
D.

16th December, 1914
8pm

Dearest Mother

Just had dinner – soup, fresh mutton, milk pudding and some of your pate de foie gras.

There is nothing to report. Yesterday we got the 113th Battery on to its target, which was a gun emplacement just at the west corner of La Bassee alongside the canal. We went and had a look at it first to see if it was occupied, and then went back over the battery and fired lights [Very signals] for them to begin firing. They apparently fired twice, but they must have fallen short in a ploughed field, as we couldn't locate them, though we were well over their lines; it is very hard to observe shells, that fall in soft plough, as they bury themselves. So, as we could make nothing of his shooting we came down and landed alongside our battery. He [battery commander] said he was very short of ammunition but that he could carry on a bit, so up we went again and this time we saw well the first 3 shots. Went left; all these we signalled and then, in their direction put the next right into the emplacement. We gave him a direct hit, and then he fairly started with all that was left of his ammunition, and fairly put them out. Low storm clouds came up almost immediately, so we went home.

[NOTE: This shortage caused a political scandal when Winston Churchill was Minister of Munitions].

On our target reconnaissance over La Bassee, we saw a long train with steam up in La Bassee station pointing for Lille. It looked as if they were filling up; also a good deal of transport on the right side of the road to Furnes and Lille. I hear our old battery commander was delighted, as he has been wanting to knock this lot out for days. I landed in a field near and it was very soft and small, young wheat, the only one available. We all thought I should have a job to get away as the wheels sank in so, but the old thing got off well.

I wish the authorities were a little more dashing in the bomb dropping business, I'm sure we could harry their lines of communications. Such big junctions as La Cateaus should be a good mark for crippling their transport.

Got cigarettes and Burberry and stockings. Will you tell the cigarette people to send me 100 each fortnight, Freibourg and Treyer, Haymarket.

Did you think to send off the Gum boots I asked for? I wonder if you got the letter – size 8½ so that I can wear two pairs of stockings, if necessary.

Today was simply vile, rain and wind all day. Went for a walk this afternoon and got drenched. I fear we are in for a wet winter. Thanks for the scarf, a fine affair. I'm really very well off for everything now, except gum boots – the cigarettes once a fortnight.

We are very snug in this wee cottage, and are all getting fat. We made a demonstration attack this morning and last night, much firing. They hope to get La Bassee soon! But how the artillery is to support, with the shortage of ammunition, I don't know, I hope they will get that right very soon.

The Daily Mail arrives too late. We can get papers now late, even the day before, so don't continue the subscription when it runs out.

Wind still howling, it is an awful night.

Much love to you and wishes for Christmas, Dearest.
From,
D.

18th December 1914.

Dearest Mother

There is nothing to report. I hear the attack on La Bassee, rather fell through, any way the French supports came back without having been engaged. I fear the trouble is shortage of artillery ammunition. I am going to observe for a battery tomorrow, that was only allowed eleven rounds of Lydite [a propellant in some shells] this morning – for the whole day!! – it's "plum ridiculous" – I heard something of this before, but was told that the shortage would soon be made up, that was more than a month ago!! The French seem all right, the 75 Battery was plugging away "Like Everythin" as White would have said. The Germans were making pretty decent shooting too dropping only 50 yards from our battery (4.7). We went out to look for a landing ground near them and climbed up a coal mound, by a disused pit that our people are using for an observation post. It was most interesting, through the glasses you could see the damage done to La Bassee Church and Givenchy – of the latter there is nothing left but one wall – also a factory chimney near has its top cut off but looking over the country what strikes you most is that there is not one living soul in sight, you have to watch very carefully and for some time with glasses before you can spot anyone, then it's fairly near, not in the advanced trenches. We saw an armoured motor car, scooting along but lost sight of it behind a wood. There was very little rifle fire – only one long artillery duel – the French 75 is quite a small gun, very neat and easily handled. They are rather exposed but the men have made wonderful shelter for themselves.

We were nearly blown off on our old coal mound the wind was that strong. I swept the horizon trying to find some troops or something on the move, not a bit of it, while the firing is going on there is absolutely not a living thing to be seen. We've got a capital landing ground there, in fact the country just about there is all good, but the field nearest the battery, the Germans have so far forgotten themselves by cutting it up with their nasty shells etc. so we put the machine behind haystacks a wee bit further back – if they go on like that, they'll end by ruining a good and convenient landing ground, for Allied aeroplanes. I fear La Bassee is still a thorn. I don't know, but we don't advance, whether it's from disinclination at the moment, or that we are unable I don't know. Went to see the French aeroplane, escadrille [squadron] at Bethune R.E.P. machines, do you remember seeing them at Buc one time coming from Fontainbleau. All was very well kept and every machine in a tent – but it's not much of a machine for war purposes.

Thanks for papers. This is a terribly dull country, very flat. Staple industry is sugar making, consequently the whole country is under beet cultivation. It's a poor climate too, wind, rainy and foggy, still we can't complain this little cottage is really quite comfy. I must say at present we can't see any end to it. Whether Germany will get the hump (when they get to know the true state of affairs), is, I suppose our chief hope but things march slowly and I should think the Rhine position is practically untakeable. Well good night, it's my bedtime.

Much love to you, dearest Mother,
D.

20th December, 1914
6.30pm

Dearest Mother,

Today has been gorgeous. Have been out all day. First
Evans and I did a tactical reconnaissance and spotted a
new battery. We were hanging about picking up details of
their position, when from quite a snug little orchard, he
started firing. I suppose he got fed up waiting for us to go
away, as generally they never fire when we are over them,
but lie dogo till the nasty aeroplane has taken itself off.
However this chap was very unwary and we got him.
Evans went off to report our landing, and this afternoon
we got the 114th Battery on to it landing just behind the
trenches. There they told us the Germans had got through
in two or three places! However it is bound to be that way.
We've probably got 'em all back by now again. But there
was some scrap going on all day; they were driving them
back out of a wood, less than half a mile off. After having
got the Battery on that target, we wanted to do another,
but it was ten to four and getting dark; but we thought
we'd just have time to do it, as it was such a fine evening
for seeing flashes. But when we had got to about 1,500 feet
we saw what I took to be a man-carrying kite, which
looked to be hovering over the Bois de Biez. We both
agreed that that was about what it was, come out at dusk
to observe our Batteries firing. So we agreed to give up the
target and go and see what manner of beast it was.

We were too low for comfort, as the Bois do Biez is
infested with anti-aircraft guns. So we climbed all we
knew, and in doing so with the nose cocked up I lost sight
of it. However, Evans said he could keep it in view, but
when they saw us coming they hauled it down. Evans had
some shots of it. Then on the other side of the wood near

Heslis we saw a sausage balloon slowly rising; so we had to go at that too, Evans plugging away, but as we neared it, it retired most amazingly fast, and as we only had a rifle, and it was getting dark, we gave it up as hopeless to damage it. We were glad enough to get it hauled down. They are captive things used by the Germans for observing artillery fire. [The Allies later used similar balloons.] We got them both hauled down. It is just possible that Evans hit them, but I fear he wouldn't do any damage to the sausage balloon.

We landed pretty well in the dark all right. It was interesting, especially seeing the flashes of the Batteries and the bursting shrapnel.

I'm thinking of trying to out-manoeuvre that sausage balloon, as I feel sure it comes out at night to observe the flashes of our Batteries.

There has been a dickens of a battle all day. I've just heard that we have those trenches back again and Givenchy.

I have never seen anything so clear as it was this morning; you could see every trench at 5,000 feet.

That target near Las [sic] Bassee is quite knocked out, they moved away, so that's good. It's wonderful looking down on the certain spots and seeing the extraordinary number of shell holes. Some parts are quite pock-marked, especially round clumps of trees, and small clusters of houses. Altogether we had a most interesting day.

I fancy the Germans have been and are making another effort here. A lot of troops were seen on the move, going and coming, between Courtrai and Menin and also this way too. Eight Battalions were seen marching to where a vast number of motor buses and lorries were parked, evidently to transport them hence, somewhere. I believe they are wonderful for getting their troops changed about

I suppose all is going for the best, but we don't get on

much, if any. Our line is Armentiere, straight line to Neuve Chapelle, thence straight line to Givenchy which has been so hardly disputed today.

Won't they let old Jock off his last month, he has nearly been three now.

Dinner time now, so stopping for food. Best love to you my dear Mother.

Ever your loving,
D

22nd December 1914

Dearest Mother,

Thank you for papers and plum pudding and books; also gum boots, the latter are splendid, I went out this morning and my feet were as warm as toasts all the time. It was a disappointing morning in one way, as the clouds were very low, but I thought it worth trying, so we went out for a tactical [reconnaissance] and got up above the clouds almost at once, it was lovely up there, and having got there I thought it worth while to go over La Bassee and Lilles to see if we could get to see through at all and though my observer kept saying "I can't see! I can't see! And there's the very dickens of a drift on" we kept on and just by Anle where the little railway makes a turn he saw perhaps 8 infantry battalions drawn up ready in reserve. We just got a glimpse through the clouds.

It was a bit of luck picking them up, as the HQ people thought it most important information, and I believe got very panicky.

We at once thought they were going to attack again at Neue [Neuve] Chapelle which is just in front of where they were, and as far as we can hear they did so late, but we are holding them alright.

Yesterday Bethune was full of troops, I was in a car and saw a whole Cavalry division going through at a canter.

A brigade of British Cavalry and the rest Native, squadron after squadron, it was a very fine sight.

We've had rather a bad time down this way lately, and they were bringing up reinforcements, but I hear we are holding them and even going on a bit.

Today, too, I hear, many troops are going through, Scots Guards, Coldstreams, etc. so things may march a bit now with their reinforcements. There are 8 battalions of German infantry, must be the lot that we picked up, about to get aboard some motor busses up N. of Lille the other day, they evidently mean to have a good try here.

I hear the Manchesters got back Givenchy with the bayonet.

We came back over the clouds, we saw our lines and down home and my observer fired off at once with the news, and came back saying it had put them into a great fuss at HQ.

I can see no end to it, heaven knows when the war will be over.

Trenchard tells me that there is still difficulty in getting machines owing to some sort of strike at home.

I and another are trying to work out a flight to Essen and back on Moranes if we get them, as we are supposed to be going to, they hold more petrol and consume less than the Bleriot, but it won't come off for some time, even if permission is given. We want to carry 6 bombs (18lb) a piece. I think it would do a bit of good morally, as to my proposed Berlin trip the petrol weight with bombs <u>was</u> the difficulty, but I was relying on a wind of certainly 50 miles an hour behind me or wouldn't have started. The Russians were to have been warned if 'they' had permitted the attempt.

The Essen trip is roughly 410 miles there and back, this would require 8 hours petrol allowing good margin.

8 hours petrol –	40 gallons –	280 (lb)
	pilot	154 (")
	bombs	82 (")
	oil	80 (")
		596 lb

and the maximum weight machine will lift is 606 lb so we are just comfortably under this.

Trenchard said he was studying maps and ways and means he didn't say what for, but I think generally, so perhaps we have stirred up something after all.

Many thanks for the papers, they are appreciated, just got cigarettes too. Am finely off for everything now.

We shall eat more than usual this Xmas, I think.

I will write to uncle when I get time to write him a good long letter.

Much love to you for Xmas, my dearest Mother,
Ever yours,
D.

P.S. I am rather bored with all this blackguarding the Germans, they can't help it, poor people, they don't know any better.

25th December, 1914
4.30pm

Dearest Mother,

Here we are Xmas day, and a lovely morning very early
though a bit misty. As we are getting ready to go out, up
came the fog, and by 9 o'clock it had got thick, by midday
you could hardly see across the road. A very sharp frost
too last night.

Yesterday we did a tactical reconnaissance and picked
up a lot of transport and two trains, but not much other
movement, at one place, infantry seemed to be detraining
from motor lorries, at Lorgies. We could only get out in the
afternoon as there was a mist in the morning. I went out as
I was not satisfied about the height of these clouds, sort of
mist and found we were in it at 300 feet! and above the
clouds at 700 in glorious sunshine, quite useless for doing
any good so down we came.

The Major told me it was lucky we saw that lot of
infantry near Anhers the other day as that evening a
sudden and most violent attack was delivered by them
between Neue [Neuve] Chapelle and Fertahert.

Today we had a very interesting reconnaissance
mapped out but it couldn't come off because of the fog.

Tonight we are all dining up at the Chateau, as a Xmas
festivity. I hear the Germans are piling in troops on the
front again and I hear confidentially from Trenchard that I
may have a mission later, but nothing is granted yet. I will
let you know further details when I know more; he is very
cheery and friendly always. I think he is delighted to get
away from F'boro. [He was now RFC field commander]

We have a lot of stuff given us, in the shape of eatables,
a ham and so forth. We are living very well indeed, eating
too much I fear, and just in from a good long walk with

another over eater. We are just going to eat again. Tea, with jam and a large cake (one of yours).

Everyone got six large cigars today and a Xmas card from the King. They were solemnly dealt out to us. The cigars were very good. Yes, I would like some if Pietro can find them or another good brand. These were Romeo and Juliette.

Will you also send me a pair of these boots [CW obviously included a description of specific footwear] size about 8 or 8½ or even 9 if the sock is very thick. I hear they are the best for warmth and for keeping you dry, my gum boots are a great success but they don't do for walking and I hear these are excellent.

I wrote to Uncle J., hope you are having a cheery Xmas.

We are doing well here, though it is cold and foggy.

I hear we are all to get Moranes later, my dear old Bleriot has been going so well.

Much love dearest Mother.
D

CHAPTER SIXTEEN

Silent Night – Hilarious Day

There were still some echoes of peacetime and civilised behaviour when Christmas 1914, the season of peace and good will, ushered out the first five months of the war. Not only did the opposing armies meet in no-man's-land to sing carols and play football together, but there was also a touch of humour in the air. During this 'festive season' a German and a British aircraft came into close contact near St. Omer. The observers in both aircraft blazed away with all they had – rifles and pistols. They soon ran out of ammunition but the German observer used his Very pistol and continued the attack with pyrotechnics. The British observer replied with flares from his signal pistol as the two aircraft came to close quarters; all to no effect. Both crews realised the futility, and indeed the fun, of it all. All four men enjoyed the joke and with no chance of achieving a kill, they fired their last flares just to add to the celebration.

There were other remnants of chivalry early on. The sky was a very large place and there were very few aircraft in the void. At that time when opposing aircraft did meet, it required a considerable amount of luck to bring an enemy plane down. There was a camaraderie among the early pilots as Lt W.S. Douglas (later Lord Douglas of Kirtleside) recalled:

A German two-seater was about 100 yards away and just below us and its observer did not appear to be shooting at us. We were completely unarmed so there was nothing to be done. We waved a hand at the enemy and proceeded with our reconnaissance task, and they did likewise. At that time this did not appear to be in any way ridiculous – there was a bond of sympathy between all who fly, even between enemies.

Later, when aircraft fitted with machine-guns firing through the propeller disc appeared in the autumn of 1915, the war in the air became more deadly.

CHAPTER SEVENTEEN

Letters: 28 December 1914 to 26 January 1915

28th December, 1914.

Dearest Mother,

This is by one who is going home. We've been getting out a bit lately, did a largish reconnaissance two days ago, saw much transport and troops entraining.

Yesterday my motor stopped, luckily over our lines, there was a very high wind indeed and I couldn't get to any good ground against it, and daren't turn tail for fear of getting too far towards the Germans so had to try and niggle down into a ploughed field surrounded by trees. Whee! We got down alright with only slight damage, the field was small and we ended up in a ditch, but there was marvellously little damage, in fact if the wind hadn't been so high and pouring rain and a ploughed field to get out of, I should have sent home for what I wanted in the shape of spare parts and flown home. However owing to the elements the whole show was carted home on a special lorry for the purpose, trouble was petrol pipe, but we had only just returned from circling over a target between La Bassee and Lens well into their lines, and if the motor had stopped then I should not have had a hope of getting into our lines "en Vol-plane" [gliding[as the wind was so strong, as it was coming from the target we took about 30 minutes to do 5 or 6 kilometres, pretty well standing quite still. The old machine has done very well and there has never been a hitch till yesterday.

Thanks for all the papers, muffler, etc. the latter is a fine one, I shall keep it and give away the other.

We can hear of no movement every day the papers say we have progressed, if this is so it is so slight, as to be almost imperceptible! We have Givenchy but that only means a few hundred yards. Some of these magazine articles you sent me are very interesting.

Today it's blowing a gale and raining!

I don't fancy they mean to advance till the spring. As one Major when at HQ t'other day, said "Please remember if we move forward, I want billets for 21 officers!" The Colonel man there said "Alright, but we are not going to advance yet."

Poor old Jock! When is he due out? 1st February will be 4 months won't it?

Well, I must stop as the sportsman is going,
Much love, dear,
From
D.

30th December, 1914

Dearest Mother

It blew a gale last night and nearly all the tent hangars blew down, chaos indescribable. Several machines broken, the poor old trailer that some of the spare wings etc. are kept in blew over too and lay forlornly with its wheels up in the air. I can never remember such a wind, two of the tents stood up, which considering the night was little short of marvellous.

We all turned out and floundered about in the mud trying to get the machines that were in the tents out before worse befell them, the two Moranes were saved. We are to get more and I may go to Paris again for one. They are very quick climbers and fast. Seventeen machines were smashed at St Omer last night, the Colonel told me, and four at Merville so the RFC has not come well out of that storm.

Tonight is calm, and looks like a frost. The weather has changed so quickly that it is hard to know what you'll get next. The tactical reconnaissance that went out today, the only one available, nearly all the others were damaged more or less, reported nothing of importance going on.

News is scarce but I hear the French are doing well and have advanced twelve miles N.E. of Mulhausen, which will put them on the Rhine. There was a very heavy cannonade over Lens way yesterday, I hear the French were attacking. We as far as one can learn are just sitting tight, my machine will be itself again tomorrow evening, I hope, it has not been touched since owing to worse fatalities to others,

Thanks for papers. Pietro sent me a card, will you thank him and say I liked it very much.

I see by the "Field" [sporting magazine] Kilkenny hounds are hunting away in South Kilkenny.

Well, I must go to bed, so night night.
Much love to you,
From
D.

———————————

New Year's Day 1915

Dearest Mother,

Such weather, yesterday was impossible and today is
rather worse if anything. My motor developed a broken
inlet valve when looked to, and a lot of the broken pieces
are, I fear, in the engine, anyway it is getting looked to
now. I told them on landing that I thought an inlet valve
had gone but the mechanics seemed to think it alright, and
this morning when I came to try it – Bang Bang! and there
we are. Still we couldn't possibly have done anything so it
doesn't matter. Clouds today are 700 feet, and very thick
and a high wind with rain squalls.

I hear the KR [Kings Royal] Rifles had a badish time
yesterday, the Germans got in and put them out, and last
night there was a counter attack on our part to regain, only
a small affair; two companies got put out. I expect with the
reinforcements they were bringing up, we have the trench
back again. The 1st Corps are here now, the Indians are
resting at Lillers [British slang for Lille].

Thanks for the cigars, I like them very much, it's a very
nice cigar.

Nothing much doing along the front, we hear good
news of the Russians and the French in the Argonne.
Trenchard hasn't said anything more about my "Mission",
I suppose they are thinking it all out. "They" take a long
time.

The Navy seems to be getting great "divarshun"
[Irishism for diversion]. I think that kind of thing does
good, it keeps the ball rolling.

I'm sure Essen, well bombed, would cause thought in
Germany, but it's a far cry from here, there and back, that's
the trouble, as you would in all probability have a stiff
wind against you one way or the other. They don't like

risking the machines as we are short as it is, still I feel more of that kind of thing should be done.

I think this continual artillery observation rather a waste of two people, one man on a single seater could do the job alright, perhaps when we get the "Morane" they'll get more lively, that seems a really useful machine and climbs wonderfully.

The Major and Cholmondeley came to dine last night in our wee cottage but we did not see the New Year in, went to bed early.

Much love to you, dear Mother, we'll hope for a happy New Year.

P.S. Old Jock comes out end of month, doesn't he?

2nd January, 1915
5.30pm

Dearest Mother,

We tried to do some Artillery [spotting for the guns] once again today, with no success; the early morning was hopeless, low clouds, wind and rain, and the very dickens of a morning, but about 12, it started to look up a bit, and we sallied forth on the chance, got badly bunked about getting off and continued to get well jerked up till 2,000 feet was reached; there was a nasty looking bank of cloud coming up fast with the wind which I could see was going to get between us and both our target and battery.

We struggled up to 4,000, but the wind was so strong and blowing straight for Germany that I thought we never would get back for La Bassee, at 4,000 we sat up there quite still, seeing the ground very occasionally through much cotton woolly cloud. After sitting there for a good while, I gave it up as my passenger began to complain that we were going backwards, turned right-handed, and edged off, coming down through very thick cloud, staggered home quite low, and even then it was some struggle, clouds very low down, and wind 60 miles an hour anything over 1,500 feet, and plenty of it still lower.

The weather is disappointing, but I suppose it's only to be expected this time of year in this 'orrible country. Russian news is cheering, here there is 'nothing to report', occasional trenches captured and recaptured again. What a life!

Here is a very rough map of our trip today. Here is a card I got from Burgre Watson. The poor old Bleriots are doing their best, but they are too slow and not suited to 60 and 70 miles an hour winds.

We are having no luck with the Moranes that have arrived two are smashed completely, we are getting them in turn I think mine is next but one. I'm looking forward to mine, they are I think, fine and efficient machines, but you must land them into the wind, directly into it, wind still moaning but there is a lovely moon, hope for a fine demain [tomorrow] . .

We have no more news, so night night.
With much love, dearest Mother,
D.
P.S. Will you send out my old fur flying short coat, the one I got at Pau, don't want new one.

———————————

5th January, 1915
6 pm

Dearest Mother,

Our old friend the weather is very bad indeed, though today it made an effort to clear and I got out beyond La Bassee and Violaines where they want to try and find some gun emplacements which are well hidden, however the motor was going so badly, that we had to give it up after doing our target reconnaissance, this is another motor and is not a good puller, lots of vibration and some misfiring, on landing they found a bearing gone, as my machine is again out of actions, owing to motor trouble, I shall take over Pretyman's machine temporarily, he is on leave. However I saw some transport this morning at the crossroads beyond La Bassee and the gunners shelled it later. Hope they put it out.

Our people are very much worried by hidden guns in what we call the 'triangle', which is a triangle made by the railways, S.E. of la Bassee.

They shell it and shell it, but still the German guns continue their attentions. We had a good look at it today at least I did when I wasn't listening to the motor 'missing' but it is hard to see where the guns are exactly, as the whole place seems a sort of rubbish heap with lots of red stuff in scattered heaps, which appear to be brick heaps.

Their guns must be in there amongst the stuff, they are going to shell one particular place, that may hit it off, as the motor was not going well we couldn't climb high, even if we wanted to, so we ought to have seen something, if there is anything in it, but my observer said afterwards that he was more concerned with the misfiring of the motor and couldn't keep his whole attention on the triangle!

We went out again this afternoon on another machine, as my motor was misbehaving, but said he [the observer] couldn't locate any guns.

I had a rather interesting talk with a battery commander. He tells me that the Germans system would appear to be infinitely better than ours, in so much that every infantry regiment has one battalion of pioneers, whose sole job is to dig trenches for their regiment, they are sent on, covered by the regiment and supported by artillery, as much as possible, and dig like badgers, then up comes the regiment well fed, well shaved and walk in to the nicely prepared trenches whereas our poor people have to dig their own trenches and then defend them or attack as the case may be, – the attacking German soldier does no digging and consequently is fresh, he also told me that the French method of attack is so good, that we are adopting it, as far as possible, he says that the artillery support is simply magnificent, that they "arroser" [spray] the ground in front of their infantry with shrapnel, like a man watering plants, then when they think there simply can't be anything living left in that area, the infantry advance with the bayonet, but the wonderful part apparently is the hail of shells.

The French Artillery Commander told him that Joffre [the French General commanding all the Allied Forces] had sent in to our General Staff, for their information, that he can get now, as much and more gun ammunition than the French can possibly use, however long the war lasts. This is distinctly cheering, wish we could say the same.

We are very short, lyddite especially. I hear the great point about this 75 of the French is that the recoil is taken up by such a good sort of shock absorber, that it is not necessary to 'lay' the gun after each shot as with our guns, consequently they can get off an enormous number of shots per minute. The gun itself is quite small, but its effect is got by its quickness of fire.

I hope to get a Morane fairly soon, the poor old Bleriots are getting tired, they've had much rough weather and work.

Please tell Uncle Julian that a remarkable fine assortment of good things arrived, everything very much appreciated, the potted meats are excellent. Thanks for papers and book and for waistcoat, don't send any more chocolate, we have literally pounds of it, it's stuff one gets tired of.

They are doing us very proud as regards boots, furry high ones for flying and fur caps, both very good articles, thanks also for the 'ski' boots, they'll do fine for wet, my gum boots are grand things, I couldn't get on without them, this country is very wet and the mud is "suffink" awful. They're putting loads of cinders on the "champs d'aviation" [flying field].

There is no news, on the front, went for a long walk this afternoon with a man called Barrett, who has done some hunting in Tipperary.

Well, au revoir,
Much love to you
From
D.

P.S. Old jock [sic] should be liberated 1st of February. Will you go down and get the poor old chap.

Madeline sent me a scarf for Xmas. I wrote to her but I doubt if its getting through. Will you write and thank her too for me.

———————

9th January, 1915
6 p.m.

Dearest Mother,

There is absolutely nothing to report, except rough stormy
weather which is rapidly "doing in" the machines already
somewhat weather worn. Today my motor was going so
badly that the poor old thing would hardly leave the
ground. However, it did just stagger off when a valve
went, this put the "hat" on things and I had to dodge trees
and almost haystacks! and landed safely in a nice open
field (plough) about a mile from the Aerodrome. Valve
was put right, I sent my observer back in a car and brought
the old thing home light, even then she was very sluggish
and the valve struck up again, however, just managed to
niggle home all right to find the other Morane standing
forlornly, wheels upwards, it had turned over on landing.
The Avro declined to leave the ground at all! So we had a
somewhat disastrous afternoon – no disastrous isn't right,
– troublesome afternoon, as though the Morane is
damaged it's not irrevocable, and no one was 'hurted'
[Irishism].

    We took some photographs the other day of the famous
"triangle" near La Bassee, which appears to be the key of
that position as I told you it is a triangle made by railways
south of the Canal and strongly held by the Germans. I
will try and get you a print of the photo, but at present
they're very confidential and for the G.S.[General Staff]
only. One of the prints was so clear you could see the
rolling stock on the lines and all sorts of detail. We've
photographed a great many of the trenches too, it's very
interesting following them out and placing them on the
map. I hear today that from T [Trenchard] that the General
has vetoed all long distance raids at present, but that later,

about the end of March, when we advance, there will be plenty of opportunity, so they evidently are not thinking of moving yet awhile! I suppose they know best. I wonder if Italy is coming in. I have a sort of feeling that the war might finish about end of June with a decisive affair about June 18th, history repeating herself 1815–1915. [1815 Waterloo] Until we can get them out of this infernal triangle we cannot advance. The gunners have been pasting it hard and I believe are going to have a regular bombardment soon, all guns turned on it, then the infantry will attack after it has been sufficiently shelled.

This gives you the position, it's a strong place and I fear will want a lot of taking. The rain has been dreadful, the whole country is more or less a marsh, and the road from the Chateau to this cottage is flooded today. Poor Picton Warlow who was here in this house with us before Xmas is missing, such a nice fellow, he started off from St Omer and has not been heard of again. I hope to get a Morane fairly soon. They are fine machines, but you must absolutely land them dead with the wind.

Madeleine sent me a scarf for Xmas, very nice soft one. When you write you might thank her for it and say I like it. I wrote to her but I doubt it's ever getting all that way these troubled times. Tell her I wrote her also. Remember old Jock comes out February 1st, poor old dog. I am afraid he hasn't had much of a time down there. Give him fine runs by the Serpentine when you get him, he loves that, barking at the things people throw in, such an old chap. Well a bientot.

Much love to you, dearest mother.
From D

10th January, 1915
7.30pm

Dearest Mother

Quite a heavy day's work today 5 hours ten minutes
Artillery observations for the Armoured train. They've
been shelling the triangle today but our first target was the
bridge across the canal just at the western end, he was
using his 6 inch gun and made some very good shooting,
hitting the southern end of the bridge, also a chance shot –
left – blew up something big, I think it must have been a
railway wagon full of ammunition on the line, anyway,
there was 'some' explosion, we were over the triangle at
the time and saw it well but it was difficult to say exactly
what it was, as shots from other batteries were falling all
round and there was much smoke from the high
explosives, they've fairly pasted it and damaged bridge
and railway and, I should imagine, smashed up everything
anyway, in the western end of it.

We got the armoured train on to target No 41. (German
gun emplacement) all right, for our second effort, using
4.7s, however, he is not so good with these but however,
he hit it in the end. Then we spotted a German battery in
some trees in a Chateau, by the flashes, a long way off
(probably they didn't see us) watching the 'triangle'
bombardment was a wonderful sight, some of the shots
fell into the canal. The Western corner is the strong place,
perhaps by now we have it took.

Thanks for letter with Phillip's letter and Times. Today
was lovely all day, we were only stopped once for a short
time owing to low driving clouds and a misty haze about
lunchtime. Tonight it's raining again, so I expect tomorrow
will not be up to sample. In off times I go for walks, it's a
queer uninteresting country. The whole country is under

beet for sugar making and so every available inch is plough land and very heavy at that. No country to ride over. I hear the fox dogs at Ypres were rather a failure as horses couldn't cross the county, it's so deep, it's all intersected with dykes and very wet and flat, there is some big woodland.

Well dinner's just coming in so bye bye. With much love. D.

13th January, 1915
4.30pm

Dearest Mother,

Am again sending this by one who is going home. He is getting lots to take so may remember to post them. The weather is still bad, though day before yesterday we were tempted out by a fine day, but the wind was so high I couldn't get home at 2,000 [feet] from the triangle. We were shooting at the Western end of it, and saw ten fair shots, then clouds came up and we had to go down to 2,000 where it was very difficult to manoevre [sic] owing to the most terrific 'secous' [shake], however, we stuck it till we bracketed out gunner on his target, this is when he has put one just over and another just short, he then knows where he is, and works up to it by process of exhaustion. I had to put the nose down all the way home to move. I crossed Bethune about 1,000 feet, we got a good shaking up, but landed safely. We were the only machine out, even the fast single seater capable of 95 miles an hour though it went out came back back as he couldn't make no headway at 4,000. Yesterday was useless and today we tried again,

but there was a very strong wind, too strong for the old
Bleriots, we stood still at La Bassee and a cloud came along
and we saw nothing more of the ground till I reckoned, we
ought to be over our lines and switched off. We should
have taken all day to get home at 4,000. Did you send
Tatler, Sketch etc. this week, I never got them. It has
poured all afternoon. Hope I'll get a Morane soon.
Yes do go and meet the old dog Jock, he will be pleased
to get out.

I don't think there is any news on this front. We did get
into the triangle but couldn't hold it, owing to enfilading
fire, it was too far advanced. Things were quiet this
morning. We commence to have enough of this 'ere war.
The paper I'm writing on is a present to our troops on
active service. Everyone got a packet, with p.c.'s
[postcards] and a pencil. Have just come in from a walk up
to, what I call, my fox cover on the hill.

Much love to you dearest mother.
D.

15th January, 1915
6pm

Dearest Mother

I walked into Bethune this afternoon, only just got back;
it's about 5 kilometres by the road, but I found a short way
across country. B is full of soldiers mostly Scotch
reinforcements going up to the trenches. We are holding
on, but not gaining anything. I had my hair cut and
shampooed, as the man said "Il etait necessaire", such a
nice clean Coiffure there, quite as good as a Paris shop,

men in white coats and everything spotless; they certainly do these things well. Went and had some coffee at the Cafe where a black-and-tan terrier lives, he came and sat beside me and ate the sugar. Two 'ouvriers' [workmen] were having the deuce of a squabble outside on the pavement, watched by an amused crowd of Highlanders, first one man gesticulating violently would walk away, closely followed by the enemy, then when he turned and faced the danger the other one would make off closely followed up in his turn; they were too ridiculous.

No aviation possible, it's blown a gale from the S.W. and clouds at 500 feet. There are quite a few good shops in B, and now you can get almost anything you want there. The streets are full of London Scottish, they are a fine lot of men, if size goes for anything. Was told off for a long reconnaissance yesterday, Lens, Douai, Lille, Menin, Amentieres, but it never came off, owing to this gale setting the wrong way. The Major thought I should never get back, and anyway the clouds were too low. I went out to see what it was like and was in cloud at 1,500 feet and standing quite still against the wind, which was in the old quarter S.W. to W., and therefore straight to the German lines, should have had it in the beam from Douai to Lille and Menin and then we should have stuck after turning for home. Both our Moranes were again out of action, and the Avro cannot be induced to leave the ground owing to the heavy going. So the old Bleriots are the mainstay still. Hope I get a Morane soon. I fear the infernal war is going to be a long job, I believe the Germans will stick at it till all's blue. Nearly our dinner hour, another meal, we do nothing but eat.

Much love to you dear.
From D.

18th January, 1915

Dearest Mother,

I hear today that my turn for a week's leave will come on
the 30th, so if nothing untoward happens, I shall cast up
then. Of course you never can tell in this kind of affair, but
if things go normally I shall be in London on the evening
of the 30th, but don't expect me until you see me actually;
this is the fourth day we have done nothing! The weather
is really vile, it snowed hard this morning and heavy
storms keep rolling up every few minutes. Two new
Moranes have come, I believe I ought to get about the next
one that comes through. I see the papers are making lots of
a success at La Bassee, we know nothing of this; things are
as they were; we did as I told you, pushed on into the
Western end of the triangle, but found we couldn't hold on
as we were too advanced and got enfiladed [fired on from
the flank], so we are back again, as we were. Still it may be
something we haven't heard of, though I think it unlikely.
It's a terrible war, everyone living underground and in
such a country, it's so wet that's the trouble. It will be nice
getting home for a week, and we can get the old dog out
too, and take him to the Serpentine. We all commence
indeed to have enough, this sitting down waiting is very
tiresome, one sees no end to it. The French appear to have
gone back a bit at Soissons, but I don't think it is very
important as they have the Aisne to negotiate.

There is absolutely no news to give you. Walked
yesterday into Bethune for something to do, and saw some
of the Camerons just out of the trenches, they were
covered in mud from head to foot and mostly with beards,
but very cheery and fit looking. I went and got a most
excellent cup of coffee at a Cafe and walked out again
across country.

This pen is giving out, so hastily bye bye.
With much love to you dearest mother.
From D.

———————————

21st January, 1915
5pm

My dearest Mother

Although today was very dull and cloudy, we did some
work. The poor old machines have been snowed and rained
on solid for five days, but this morning, though cloudy, was
fine. I went out alone to see what it was like, and though
there was a lot of low lying clouds, it was clear enough in
patches. I went out over the triangle to La Bassee to see if the
pontoon bridge was blown up, as the 26th Liege [Regiment]
reported they had done it in, but all bridges were intact.
Came back to report, and then went out again with an
observer, to look for the German armoured train and some
gun emplacements they want to know about. Did the whole
thing about 3,000, and even then we were in cloud a lot of
the time. Didn't see Mr Armoured Train, but spotted about
50 motor 'buses on the move between Salome and La
Bassee, evidently about 2 regiments coming up to reinforce.
My observer thought he spotted a gun on a pontoon bridge
at La Bassee. Ran into cloud and saw nothing more till
nearly back at Bethune. Lots of drift while in clouds.
Observer new to the job and a little jumpy. This afternoon it
clouded up completely very low down, quite hopeless. It's
raining again hard now. The country gets wetter and wetter
each time one flies over it there is more water out.
    I'm wondering what became of my motor 'buses today,
as a Morane was sent out, on our reporting, to see if he

could discover where they were parked, but failed to find any trace of them, but cloud worried him too. All that rubbish in the papers about great British success at La Bassee is all rot, we have not advanced. Same old shelling goes on and that's about all. Occasionally a trench is won or lost, but there is such a network of trenches now that they pretty well all connect German and British. This is an underground war, consisting of artillery duels and burrowing in the earth. hope to get away on the 30th, as I told you, if all goes well. Yes, it was a wretched business about Picton-Warlow; he was going home to instruct new pilots in the Bleriot. Such a nice fellow.

We hear there are lots of new pilots coming out, and the place is stiff with new observers. Well a bientot I hope.

With much love to you,
D.
Thanks for papers.

23rd January, 1915
5.45pm

Dearest Mother,

There has been much cannonading all day; the wind has changed so that now the big guns shake this cottage and make our windows rattle. Generally with the prevailing wind S.W. we hardly hear them at all. But the wind has gone into the E. veering to N.E. and the last two days have been gorgeously fine, but very hazy on the ground; sharp frost last night.

I've done nothing today, owing to my motor going wrong 'on me'. It chose beyond La Bassee (Salome) to give out in one cylinder and we staggered home on 6. Motor has to be changed. We were rather having fun, as it was cloudy, filmy sort of stuff that kept coming along and covering us and then clearing off and letting us see beautifully. It kept worrying the local 'Archibalds' and the old 'How' [howitzer] at La Bassee, who is very slow, and I'm glad to say up to now rather indifferent. We were out looking for gun emplacements, moving generally; saw them changing their guns at one place. We were never more than 2,500 feet, and could hear the rifle fire very distinctly. They are going back slightly, and so I think are we, to get out of the water, which now fills all the trenches; they are putting their men into redoubts, dotted about, and we are doing likewise, as really the trenches must be uninhabitable. There is water out everywhere. I will try and get some photos to bring home.

The old Bleriots are pretty well done. I believe they are going to condemn them, poor old things; they've done good service.

The strategical reconnaissance reported little or no movement behind Lille today, a few supply trains, but nothing important. I suppose it's a sort of 'Who gets tired first' kind of job now.

Having nothing to do today I went out for, what is known as a 'joy ride' in a Morane Parasol, the pilot took me over Bethune for an airing. I enjoyed it, you see wonderfully from the machine, as the plane [wing] is over your head, and so you get a clear and uninterrupted view in all directions.

There is no news; both are pretty well stuck in the mud I should imaging [sic]; it's quite the worst mud you ever saw.

Well, a bientot, I hope to be home on or about the 30th.

Much love to you, dear Mother,
D.

26th January, 1915

My dearest Mother,

Calm, foggy weather for three days. This morning looked a little better and tempted me out, but found clouds at 1000 feet, especially thick over the lines, so gave it up as useless. This afternoon it came down thicker than ever.

Yesterday the Germans got through at Givenchy, but we drove them out again later, killing 4,000. We, I fear, also must have lost heavily, especially the Black Watch.

Hope Evans is all right, he used to come out in the 'Tactical' with me very often when he was observing here. He went back to his regiment, as they wanted him, owing to shortage of officers.

They shelled Bethune slightly yesterday, but with little or no damage. There was, however, a really terrific cannonade joining in yesterday morning between seven and nine. We could easily distinguish the 'yap' of the French 75's which appears to have fired unceasingly for more than two hours. It was really marvellous how continuous they were. It is something to have ammunition like that. Our heavy artillery kept booming away, more slowly and sedately, intermixed with the popping of hand Grenades, rifle fire, and the peculiar noise of the German high explosive bursting, in reply. Pandemonium! 'They' lost 4,000 in that attack, and are back again, and not a wit 'forrader' [forward]. Went out to see what was doing, but could see nothing owing to fog over the lines. I think it is partly caused by the marshy state of the ground. Anyway whenever there is a slight fog here, it's generally sure to be pretty thick over yonder.

I went out to dine with Trenchard last night in his magnificent chateau beyond Lille. He was very cheery, and asked after you and how you liked the journey back from

Italy. Everyone seems to think that was a great effort. He tells me we are getting ten more Moranes.

Took out a new observer this morning, Captain Povah, the poor man couldn't see 'nuthin', of course, much disappointment, as it was his first time out over the lines. The place is stiff with new observers who have to be taught. Thanks for photos, they are very good, also for papers.

Yes, I hope to be home on the 30th, but have not heard definitely yet. We are, I fancy, rather short of pilots. The flat looks very nice indeed. Nice balcony for Jock to air himself and watch the passing world.

I shall now go and post this and then go for a short walk before tea. Much love to you, dearest of Mothers.

Your loving,
D.

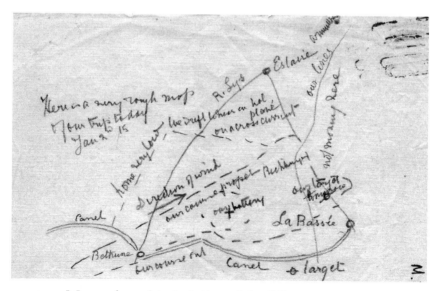

Map referred to in letter of the 2 January, 1915.

CHAPTER EIGHTEEN

Moranes, at Last!

In December 1914 the French-built Morane-Saulnier Type L 'Parasol'began to arrive spasmodically at No. 3 Squadron. They gradually replaced the ageing Bleriots that had been the squadron's mainstay since coming to France. It then had seven whose number was increased direct from the factory. But by now all were war-weary, mainly due to the lack of proper hangarage and their lack of robustness for field duty.

The wing of the Morane was of orthodox wood-and-fabric construction; there was a large cut-out in the trailing edge above the observer's cockpit. Wing warping was still the means of lateral control. The fuselage was a wooden wire-braced box girder which tapered to a horizontal knife-edge; the front panels were of plywood and the remainder was fabric-covered. The elevators and the rudder were remarkably small in area and there was no fixed fin. But as production of the Type L continued there were various modifications that culminated in the Type LA, which gradually superseded the earlier type in No. 3 Squadron.

The first Morane had been delivered direct to the squadron on 2 December, but it lasted only a week before it was wrecked. Three more were supplied but though No.3 had been given preference for deliveries, it was still somewhat under strength, having written off a total of four before the year ended.

CW ended his home leave via Paris where he rendezvoused with Lt Hanlon and Sgt. Dunn to collect three more. This type L had evolved from earlier Morane shoulder-type monoplanes, a few had served in the pre-war RFC. Corbett Wilson had flown some of these at Farnborough and was quite enamoured of them except for their tricky landing properties which he frequently mentioned in the early letters. Generally their pilots considered them to be good, if somewhat unspectacular: this being put down to a combination of sluggish lateral control (wing warping was still used) and an over-sensitive reaction from the elevators. Nevertheless, it was a Morane Type L of No. 3 Squadron that gave the RFC one of its earliest combat successes. On 5 February, 2nd Lt Wadham and his observer, Lt Bourton encountered an enemy Aviatik which Bourton drove down to earth with the skilful use of his rifle, his concluding shots being fired at a range of only 50 feet.

The Morane Type L lasted for about a year until, at the end of 1915, Major General Trenchard signalled the Military Aeronautics Board 'I am sending home as soon as possible the remainder of the old type (warped wings) Morane parasols for instructional purposes'. As these had no dual control and needed considerable skills in handling, their use as trainers must have been very limited. As production of Type L continued there were various improvements, including ailerons, which culminated in the Type LA with which No. 3 Squadron was eventually completely re-equipped.

But in the meantime CW had his own views on the Type L, which he expressed in the following letters.

The problems with the 80hp Le Rhone engines were resolved – almost – when a number of mechanics, including James McCudden, from No. 3 Squadron completed a course at the engine works in Paris.

CHAPTER NINETEEN

Letters: 6 to 17 February 1915

Hotel Ritz,
Place Vendome,
Paris.
6th February, 1915.
6.45 p.m.

Dearest Mother,

Here I am installed in my suite. With difficulty I saw
Valentine today; I was not able to catch him till midday
and then he said that, as it was raining it wasn't worth
going out to the machine today, but that he would take me
out "demain" [tomorrow]. Apparently motors are the
difficulty; he has two out working and one broken down –
so that if it had been fine, I don't know how we were going
to get away. I suppose he will have one for tomorrow. The
ground has been altered and is at Le Bourget N.E. of Paris
[this site became the main Paris airport and remained so
until after the Second World War – it is still an operational
airport].

Paris seems quite full. I passed the Castelioque today
and had a chat with Bayo. He is just off to serve. He does
not know if he will go to the front.

139

We took from 8.20 to 9 p.m. to get here yesterday but it is quite a comfy journey. The train goes all round and about. I looked out once and found we were at Eu, which is, of course, miles off the regular route.

Things seem almost normal here now and Paris is full of civilians. I heard at Boulogne that we had taken Ostend, but have had no confirmation of this.

Yesterday was a lovely day. We had a most peaceful crossing, "Aucune sous-marin dans le dos"! [no U-boats were on the prowl] and quite calm. It is raining again. Valentine is to telephone what time he is coming tomorrow; I expect I shall only try the machine, as I want to get in some practice on it, before finally pushing off. Shall probably leave Monday.

No news tonight in the evening papers but anyway the news is always very old, even compared to ours. This hotel seems fairly full to judge by the number of boxes in the corridors, some of them of gigantic proportions, I suppose American. [The United States had yet to enter the war.]

Valentine is now a Captain and I think rather on his dignity, as he told me at lunch that he had been having a lot of trouble with the navy as he could not get the naval man here to acknowledge his superiority! Today, I fancy, a crisis was reached owing to a naval lieutenant proposing to go and see General Hirchauer, the French director of aviation, on a matter of business, without first consulting our friend V, who, he tells me, is "in charge" here, and so should have been approached first, or some such rubbish. He was quite amusing.

Well bye bye, dear Mother,
With much love,
D.
P.S. Love to Jock.

9th February, 1915

Machine is ready, but as it has rained solid all day, I'm still here. Shall probably get away tomorrow. Just in from motoring out on the road to Chantilly, looking for a broken down aeroplane, but when we got out there, we found he'd put out for home; he had been out all night, with some petrol trouble, but had got off just ten minutes before we arrived!! Toujours comme ca. [Things don't change.]

Love from
D.

———————

Amiens 12th February, 1915

Landed here this afternoon with misfiring motor. Am getting one of the motor Rhone specialists to come and look at it, as it persists in missing, and sometimes it chucks it altogether, and then picks up again. It was missing all the way from Paris. Had a nice flight but for that. There is a French escadrille [squadron] near and they have mechanics who understand the Rhone they are sending me out.

Love from
D.

———————

Amiens 13th February, 1915

Still here, the mechanic found something radically wrong with the Magneto; it's a wonder that the motor lasted to here; he has put things right, I hope. We tried the motor, and all went well. But it rained all day, and blew a gale, so we are still here.

I think this rather quaint.
Love to you from
D.

Grand Hotel du Rhin,
Amiens.   14th February, 1915.

Dearest Mother,

Most awful weather; it's blown a gale and rained all yesterday and again today. Three of us are held up here, Sergeant Dunn and Hanlan and myself, – all with new Moranes, which luckily are well sheltered in the good solid French hangars it's just as well we couldn't get in, as at Bethune our nice new machines would have had all this rain – to say nothing of being blown over by the wind. It was a real tempest last night, and this morning; it's moderated a bit now, but rains continuously. Yesterday I thought I'd try and start in the afternoon when it looked a little better, but though the mechanics held it, the machine blew over on to its right wing, but has done no damage that I can see. Then they told me that they had just telephoned to St. Pol, and that it was raining there, so I gave it up. I believe years ago we stayed in this hotel. I know we came here. I've been since but only to lunch, motoring through. This place is full of French soldiers, and last night a General was dining here, and everyone stood up when he left the table.

    Fortunately there are four good hangars at the landing

ground – one permanent and three portable, put there by the French merely for the convenience of people coming and going. There is no military aviation here – in this respect they do things better than we, who for three months have had our machines in the open. We shall not go out till it clears a bit, as the machines are well where they are, and as long as no work is possible they may as well remain under shelter.

I enclose a paper I bought today, also a postcard of German Infantry passing through this town. I told you yesterday, I think, that the Rhone mechanic came and thinks all will now be well, we tried the motor, and all seemed all right. I had great luck not to have crash en route; it was great luck that the French had a 'specialiste' within call. They have a camp de revitaillement aviation [aeroplane repair base], 9 kilometers from here. I could have got a new motor if I'd wanted!

Well, good-night, dearest Mother. Much love to you, D.

15th February, 1915

Dearest Mother,

Well, I've arrived at last. This morning was fine, so we motored out to the ground. I had my machine out, and started away – still misfiring. I did two or three turns round but it got worse if anything, so landed, and started the old business all over again. Did everything I could, and as it was still no better, telephoned for the mechanic, who came and changed the magneto, gave me some fresh plugs, and about 3pm, I got away all right, but by that time nasty looking storms were coming up and the wind had got up stormy, had to do most of the way at 1,000 feet to avoid cloud, ran through a snowstorm, most unpleasant, but got here all right about 4pm. Found everything much the same here.

We've got some hangars (tent) now, which is an improvement. Everyone seemed pleased to see me, which was nice. The Major very cheery. I told him that I thought things might be better now at Paris, our friend V. is quite useless and alas is, I fear, not a sahib [gentleman]. We ought to have some of our new mechanics down there to hand over machines <u>properly</u> tuned up, to any pilots coming down for machines. I left Paris with a misfiring motor, hoping it would pick up, as I knew it was no earthly use asking the ruffians who were supposed to be in charge of our machines, to do anything more than take out the plugs and clean them. This had already been done several times.

News appears of the nothing-to-report order. We've got the whole flight of Moranes here now; they are nice machines, but want knowing. Glad old Jock is well, take him to the Serpentine; he loves it.

Very sleepy. Night night, dear Mother.
Much love to you.
D.

NOTE: CW's view of the French mechanics had changed . . . but with good reason.

17th February, 1915

Dearest Mother,

Such weather! It's rained all day, and blown one gale of wind. Yesterday was lovely, was out three times. I like the machine awfully – it wants a bit of knowing, especially to land it nicely.

In the afternoon I took one of the new observers out. He succeeded in quite losing himself, poor man, and waved me out to the right. I went as I thought perhaps he wanted to see something not on our programme, and turned back when I thought he must have seen all he wanted. Not a bit of it; he still wanted to go a bit right-handed, but knowing it was out of our beat, I shook my head, and then up came a piece of paper with "Dan Station" written on it. He was miles from it, so I took him back and showed it him. However, there was very little doing: one train. Nothing doing towards Lille or beyond. Things are quiet here now. I fear my teeth are going to give trouble; the wind touched them up yesterday. [see note] Thanks for the books. The cigars arrived all right. Things have been quite at a standstill; there is no talk of a move. Goodness knows when we shall make a push – the Germans are fortifying every available place on their line of retreat beginning with Lille; they will take some shifting. Raids are apparently off, as they say they are short of pilots, but they don't use their pilots for anything useful except this usual infernal reconnaissance where everyone is underground, and you seldom or never see a living thing on the move between daylight and dark.

I'm tired of asking to do things; there is only a lot of talk and nothing ever comes of it. Heard Terrence is going into the RFC – they want gentlemen [a further snobbish reference to "us and them"]!

Well, I'm very sleepy, so I shall toddle off to bed. It's blowing great guns and still raining.

Much love to you, dear Mother,
Ever your loving,
D.

NOTE: CW got back to London for dental treatment and stayed at his mother's Knightsbridge apartment, 3 Hans Place. He had to have 16 teeth extracted – dental conservation was a long way off!

CHAPTER TWENTY

The First Battle

T he battles of the early months of 1914 were not 'battles' in the sense that they are thought of today. From the British point of view, Mons, the Marne and the Aisne were rather struggles for survival. By January 1915 the BEF Commander, Sir John French, was planning a Spring Offensive and he needed a clear picture showing the intricacies of the enemy's trench system. For this he depended on photographic sorties undertaken by the RFC in early February. Using a new aerial box camera manufactured to the Corps' specification, the aviators had photographed the whole German trench system and built up a detailed mosaic of the area that the ground troops faced. The Germans held a salient centred on the village of Neuve Chapelle and its elimination was the first objective of the offensive. Neuve Chapelle was the first land battle in which an air force played a closely-integrated part during the three days that it lasted.

As the official RFC history records:

For the first time ever, the British Army went into action with a picture already passed into legend. The first months of 1915 were a time of hope, of wide-ranging plans and far-reaching ideas which were destined to end, at best, in stalemate or in another gallant litany of fortitude and loss.

Neuve Chapelle would be something new – it was hoped. The RFC would contribute more than just photographs: bombing, reconnaissance, and artillery co-operation would play a vital role. All three Wings (a third one had been formed) would be committed; apart from the Germans the main enemy would be bad weather.

On the morning of 10 March three machines from No. 3 Squadron began the softening-up process, dropping bombs from as low as 100 ft. The air offensive continued but against formidable opposition and the danger of 'own goals' from the British artillery. Lt D.S. Lewis, Royal Engineers attached to the RFC reported:

> I saw most of it from the air and I was badly scared. We had about 400 guns all firing like hell and as we were flying at about 1,200 feet, owing to clouds, we were fairly surrounded by our own shells. It was quite a relief crossing the line to exchange German bullets for British shells. No troops would have withstood that bombardment. I fairly had the wind put up me by seeing a 9.2 inch shell whiz past my tail; two of my subalterns were killed by a shell. Owing to the weather we couldn't do much in the way of ranging but we caught most of their batteries firing which was quite useful. The first part of the show was well run: we had been registering all the batteries at all important points and every inch of the trenches had been photographed from above so that every subaltern knew exactly where he was attacking and what trenches there were in front and to the flanks.

One heartening piece of intelligence came from the pilots vigilantly patrolling the skies beyond the salient who reported no large-scale troop movements, no unusual numbers of trains rushing towards the German railhead and no fresh divisions making for the Front.

During the battle, none of No. 3 Squadron's aircraft was lost in the air but there was disaster on the ground. When a Morane was being loaded with six bombs, two of them exploded and left a dozen men lying around, badly mutilated, with the pilot dead in his cockpit. The aircraft was on fire and there were still bombs on board, so helpers quickly got the wounded away at considerable risk to themselves. It was a very bad day for the squadron for the eventual toll was eleven killed and two wounded, some of whom were very experienced aircrew.

The accident was witnessed by a sergeant mechanic, James McCudden:

> I ran over to render assistance and found about a dozen men lying around the Morane, all badly mutilated. Owing to the Morane being on fire and still more bombs being in the machine we got away the wounded quickly. I well remember the little band of helpers who assisted to get the living away from the burning wreckage at imminent risk of their own lives . . .

The Squadron CO, Major J.M. Salmond, ordered everyone to retire from the scene and with the help of an NCO he cleared away all the wreckage – an action that further endeared him to all his men.

From his early army days Major J.M. Salmond had been a convinced advocate of the use of aircraft in war. In 1910, while serving with the 2nd Battalion of the King's Own Regiment he had, in a lengthy essay, expounded the merits of reconnaissance aeroplanes operating ahead of strategic cavalry. He visualised a light aircraft for reconnaissance and a faster type for combat. He saw no difficulty in the latter type being equipped with machine-guns, yet four years later pilots were still firing at enemy aircraft with rifles and revolvers. This energetic officer would later become Marshal of the Royal Air Force, Sir John Salmond.

James McCudden had been a bugle boy and transferred to the RFC on its formation; later he became an outstanding air ace. He maintained CW's aircraft and often flew with him as his observer. In his book *Five Years in the RFC* he gave first-hand views of the dangers posed by the extremely accurate German AA fire:

> Every pilot and observer knew and respected the AA section at Fournes, and our pilots named the section gunner 'the 99-year-old gunner' as he was a good shot. Another AA gun which was rather respected was a converted Howitzer, which fired above the area of Violanes, Auchy and La Bassee. This gun fired one big shell about every 10 seconds, and its projectiles always made a double report and burst – it was nicknamed the Old How. [CW also mentions this strange weapon in one of his letters.]

The struggle for Neuve Chapelle petered out after three days with minimal gains for the BEF. During it, James McCudden, who had often witnessed German anti-aircraft fire while flying, described the effect of accurate AA fire as seen from the ground during this period:

> Our aerodrome at Donneham was only seven miles from the nearest part of the line, and in the clear spring evenings we could follow with our own eyesight our machines until they were being 'Archied' over the trenches. On some evenings we could see a river of white shell-bursts from south of Armentieres, almost down to Lens.
>
> On March 8th, Capt. Conran and Lt Woodiwiss had gone out to drop some bombs south-east of La Bassee. They arrived back in 40 minutes and as they were landing I noticed some flying wires dangling and a stream of petrol running from the machine. I ran to the Morane and found Capt. Conran badly wounded in the back and arm. We got him out of the machine and he was just about done. One shrapnel ball had embedded itself in his right arm and the

other had gone in at the side and come out very near his spine. The machine, No. 1872, was literally riddled with shrapnel and how the observer escaped unhurt I do not know for there were shrapnel marks all around him.

The shrapnel bullets each left a thin line of smoke so that each shell burst appeared as a fan which had a most effective spread. These were considered by the airmen as far more dangerous than the high-explosive shells which the Germans used later on.

CHAPTER TWENTY-ONE

Letters:
26 April to 9 May 1915

Same old place.   26th April, 1915
No.3 Squadron, RFC.

Most dear Mother,

Me voila [here I am] once more, I only stayed a couple of
hours in Farnboro', just time to get lunch and have the
machine got ready. I then packed off and did not land at
all. Had rather a bumpy trip at times, but the crossing was
delightful, so clear that I could see Cape Gris Nez from
almost Ashford. I passed over Sandgate and must have
gone over very near Christalle's house. Everything was so
clear and the crossing seemed nothing at all, as I saw the
other side so plainly. I took one hour 55 minutes from
Farnboro' to St Omer, where I went and stayed the night at
our old billet, kind people who made me very comfy.
Came on here yesterday afternoon by car as the machine I
brought was not intended for this Squadron. It was a nice
little machine and climbed well. I liked it.
    Loftus Bryan saw me off and we managed to get all my
kit in with exception of those boots and pillows, which you
might send me, not the boots, I mean the pillow, also
you might send my gum boots and that washing

underclothing I left behind. I'm back with the same flight and am to have a "Parasol Morane" like the one I brought, it seems years ago, from Paris. You might also send me 100 cigarettes every fortnight, either those you 'uster' [used to] send or Pera, 15 New Bond Street. Things are very quiet here since Neuve Chappelle, but they talk of a push being made very soon. Quien sabe? [who knows?]

Every one is very kind to me, and am settled back in our old cottage. It's a lovely morning, but C Flight has nothing to do apparently, so I have not yet tried to run my machine. Everything seems exactly the same, only people have changed about a bit, and there is only one man here in the cottage who was with me here before. I don't think the trees and hedges are much, if any more advanced than over in England, they also have had lovely weather over here. You might send me some more writing paper and envelopes. I found our late Squadron Commander, Salmond, in command at Farnboro', a man called Lewis is doing his job here. Trenchard is still Wing Commander [of No. 1 Wing]. Same old guns are booming away, but that's about all there has been to it, for some time past around here. We've got a couple of terriers here now and these fellows go out ratting and generally drawing the countryside with them.

It was funny flying over between Sandgate and Folkestone. I saw, of course, the Metropole quite well. I didn't think that time last week, that next I should be flying over that ground so soon that we used to promenade on. Well I must go off up to the ground and see what's doing.

My best love to you dear, dear Mother.
Ever your loving, D.
Love to my jobbles Jock.

No 3 Squadron, RFC   27th April, 1915

Dearest Mother,

Well, I've tried the machine and like it very much. It climbs very fast and is quite a nice affair. Today is hopeless, foggy, with low clouds.

I saw Trenchard yesterday, who was very nice and said he was glad to see me back, as there was much work to do. But things seem very quiet here just now, though we were to have made the push yesterday had all gone well, but this affair north of Ypres played Old Harry with the plans, and will put the whole advance back some time. Apparently the French territorials decamped. It was a bit of bad luck for us, as some British regiments were to have relieved the aforesaid French Territorials that very night. I suppose the Germans knew this and put up the attack before and put them out. It has consequently delayed things, as all the ground lost has to be won back. But the news from there was good last night, things are going well, and we are getting back the ground all right.

Do you remember some time ago going to Harrod's to get a camp bed with me? I'm sure we did. Well, it has never arrived. Would you find out about it?

It was bad luck, wasn't it, this delayed advance? We hear so much of it; I am beginning to think we never shall.

Much love to you, dear mother,
Ever your loving,
DEN.

April 29th, 1915
7.30am

Dearest Mother,

Am just in from Tactical reconnaissance. We left the
ground 4.55. The most gorgeous morning, though hard to
see towards the sun owing to haze, and were out fifty
minutes. It was really very pleasant though on arrival the
mechanic found a large bullet hole in the back petrol tank,
luckily we were not using it as the front tank holds
enough for the Tactical. I heard something hit the
machine when we were between Fromelles and Aubers,
but did not think much about it; we did the usual round,
passing north of the Bois de Biez, Aubers, Fromelles,
across to Wavrin, our stations, La Bassee, and home. Last
evening I did the same round, saw only one train this
morning and one last night; there is very little on the
move. I haven't heard any news this morning. I am glad
the summer is coming; it's so much pleasanter in every
way. Today is going to be hot.

Will you send me out a ham (York) like the last from
Paxton and Whitfield, Jermyn Street? It's lovely here, this
cottage gets all the morning sun. I shouldn't be surprised if
we were in for a hot summer.

Will you also send me out those old Field boots, they
are the ones I used to ride in, in Ireland; they lace up the
front and are very deep colour, almost black; not the light
brown polo boots; they are probably with them, but the
real old pair that lace up much further, and are easier to
put on.

There's a battalion of Scots Guards close by, and they
come in and pass the time of day, a good deal, very nice
people.

I expect the drawing-room at the flat looks very smart by now.

Well, bye-bye for now.
Much love to you, dear Mother.
D.

May 1st, 1915

Dearest Mother,

Only just a line to say do not send the camp bed as I have bought one out here. The only other thing I thought of was my brown shoes, the stout broad-soled ones, dark brown. Will you send these?

It is very hot, perfect weather. Yesterday we pursued a Hun airman but he put out for home before we got anywhere near him and went down to Lille.

I took some photos yesterday, Luzieres cross roads, north of La Bassee. I have not got the knack of landing this machine [the Morane L] to my satisfaction yet. It lands very fast especially when there is no wind to steady it on landing.

I have nothing to do today, so shall go out and practise – I wish we could see some ending to this infernal war; they tell us there were 20,000 casualties at this last affair north of Ypres. Ypres was burning last evening as we came home. It was clear and we could see quite well. We are living exactly the same life from day to day. In my next letter I will send Pietro a cheque for at least half of the wine bill.

With much love to you my dear mother,

Your loving,
D.
P.S. Please send me some <u>thin</u> underclothing – <u>short</u> drawers.

3rd May, 1915

Dearest Mother,

Just home from doing a Tactical reconnaissance, such an hour! It only takes about fifty minutes to one hour to do – and it is a very long time to lunch time! We shall have some breakfast about seven, generally fish and bacon and eggs. We only have some tea and a biscuit before pushing off.

It is a lovely clear morning, with a coldish Northerly wind. We had quite a nice trip round, apart from trains in different stations, my observer does not appear to have seen much. We got a new gun pit, at Herlies, saw the trail of a gun sticking out, evidently overlooked by our friends the Huns as all the rest were hidden.

Thanks for the underclothing but I shall soon want thin stuff now. We heard a tremendous bombardment Ypres way last evening. I suppose we shall hear soon the result of it – whether it was on the Germans I do not know but for more than an hour it was very severe.

The Scots Guards who were here left last evening for the trenches – a fine looking lot and seemed very cheery at going up again. This country begins to look quite nice, trees are out nearly and everything looks very green and springlike. The weather changes as regards temperature very suddenly. The last few days have been hot and today there is an icy wind. Last evening our old friend, the

Scotch mist rolled up from the sea, but it has all cleared this morning. I asked you to get a ham at Paxton and Whitfield in Jermyn Street. Will you also send me a few pots of potted meat and some of those plums. I enclose a cheque for £16, half of Pietro's bill for wine. I will send the rest later.

Much love to you my dearest mother. I am sure the drawing room does look nice.

D.

5th May, 1915

My dearest Mother

Yesterday and today have been misty, nothing could be done. Last night we got the thunder storm which had been brewing all day, it was stiflingly hot with great masses of black evil looking cloud. Away towards Lille about 6.30 we got it fairly, with a deluge. We motored into Bethune in the afternoon and walked out only just getting in in time. Bethune is quite itself again, you can almost get anything there now. It's chock-a-block with soldiers, a sprinkling of French but mostly ours.

I saw some Spahi [Splendid French Colonial Cavalry from North Africa] officers who wear brilliant red jackets with gold braid and light blue trousers, brilliant people amongst all the khaki. The day before I did the tactical reconnaissance and two hours artillery observation in the evening for a field battery near St. Vaast which meant circling round and round over the Bois de Biez, they did not shoot well, but all the same we did two targets. It's a steamy sort of day today with mist and low cloud. Perhaps our old friend the thunderstorm is coming back.

Much love to you,
D.

———————————————

7th May, 1915

Dearest Mother

There is much rumour going about that "the day", our day, is due, and that a general big push is about to come off. Anyone in any sort of authority is mysterious, and we really think that it is coming off at last; as I understand it, the plan is to attack on a front of about 3,000 yds, opposite here, with four objectives from here to Lille, the first being the Estaires, La Bassee road. I believe they reckon four days fighting from here to Lille. I don't think we shall move from here till they are well beyond Lille, but if perchance you don't hear from me, you'll know it's because we are on the move at last.

The Sussex regiment, who were resting out here, got orders to be ready in half an hour if necessary, and yesterday they moved up, in support. Of course it may all come to nothing, but it really looks like business. We are having a very peaceful quite time, as the fog is very persistent, with misty foggy sort of clouds at 2,000 feet and 1,500, – anyway I've nothing to do today, though they hint at much work soon.

Will you send me out some thin underclothing (short drawers). Funnily enough the bed from Harrod's has turned up, and I've got it. I sold the other one for what I gave for it. The new one is very comfy, so that's all right.

It's hot and steamy, but very pleasant here in our little orchard where we've rigged up a tent shelter, and have all our meals out. Fog seems getting thicker, a machine is just coming in, he has found work impossible I expect.

Much love to you, my dear Mother.
From D

THE LAST LETTER

May 9th, 1915

My Dearest Mother,

Well, the great attack is proceeding; it started at five in the morning, and I never thought to see such a sight. I was out from 5 to 7 observing for effect for a group of Batteries, and had a wonderful view of the bombardment; that was to commence operations.

Our targets were just SW of the Bois de Biez, and the shooting along the whole line was simply wonderful, if you can imagine the whole German line of trenches getting an absolutely continuous shower of high explosive and shrapnel, you have it. It never ceased for two hours, the big 45-inch howitzer was in one group, and to see its shots was extraordinary. They call it 'Granny' and the 9.2 'Mother'. Well, I saw Granny hit various things, one the Distillery, just on the Estaire La Basse road between Bois de Biez and Violaina, a huge cloud of yellow smoke enveloped the whole thing after the shot and there is no more distillery! I saw it hitting Aubers, all over the place. Also Fromelles, but what impressed me most was the continuous and never ceasing hail of shrapnel and high explosives that kept bursting right in the German trenches and on such a lovely morning, too; it was really terrible.

La Bassee has been well shelled and the old church tower is no more. Everything is burning, every house, farm and cottage – the country is so pockmarked with shells that it is literally altering the whole face of the landscape. Our batteries have all shot well; in fact I think they did all along the line. The four Corps got through first, they were N of the Bois de Biez, they got on as expected, but the Indian Corps and the 1st Corps were hung up all morning owing I expect to wire, but don't know; anyway, we hear they are through now, but a second bombardment was necessary. I believe the plan is to bombard all night and then rush the next position at dawn. We know no details, but the authorities here seem cheerful. If the Germans continue to stick this bombardment they are stout fellows. I've never dreamt of such an inferno, in my worst nightmares.

This evening I did two hours tactical reconnaissance and saw several trains on the move; one a gun train moving up to Don. Also a chateau which I think holds a regiment of Cavalry. Lots of trains in Don, and generally some movement, not much doing towards Lille. I don't think for a minute the Germans will stand this awful bombardment, that they will go back now is, I think, the general opinion. We hear the French are through on their side of the canal in two places, and that they are doing their best, I will let you know details later. Very high wind today, but perfect for seeing.

Thanks for potted meats etc., will you send the ham from P&W Jermyn Street, also some cigars, and thin blue underclothing? I shall want it. Send my love to Madeleine, if you write.

It is rather wonderful come to think of it, that this is the greatest battle I suppose the world has ever seen, and surely the greatest bombardment, and I saw it from the front of the stalls, high above it all in my little old aeroplane.

Well, I'm weary, so good night, dear Mother.
Ever your loving,
D

CHAPTER TWENTY-TWO

The Last Battle

By the first week of May Capt. Conran's Morane had been fully repaired and was allotted to CW. McCudden went up with him on its first test and was amazed by its climbing ability. After Neuve Chapelle the stalemate set in again but No. 3 Squadron continued to be very active. CW bombed a chateau and strafed enemy support and communications trenches from a low altitude, but he could not follow the ground activity because there was so much smoke – much of it generated by the Allied artillery. Bombing and strafing continued too, though the limited effect of bombing was now being re-examined.

Early on 10 May CW and 2nd Lt Woodiwiss took off on a routine flight to observe for the guns. Their aircraft was Bleriot No. 1872, in which the latter had narrowly escaped a few days earlier. When they were over Fournes disaster struck. First reports indicated that the two airmen had been pestering the Germans by throwing hand grenades on them and that one grenade had caught in the rigging of their Morane and exploded. But that was not the case. The "99-year old gunner" whose accuracy was well respected in No. 3 Squadron, had found his mark and a direct hit sent the wrecked aircraft and its occupants plummeting to earth. Woodiwiss did not escape this time, and neither did Denys Corbett Wilson.

Newton Woodiwiss had been a cadet at Sandhurst, but at the outbreak of war he had been hurriedly commissioned into his local regiment. He was keen on photography and when he volunteered for the RFC his hobby was ideal for the work in which No. 3 Squadron was engaged. He had escaped one accident early in March and miraculously a second one in early May (described earlier) when his pilot was badly wounded. Woodiwiss was only 18 years of age when the ever-increasing tempo of the air war had brought his life and that of CW to an untimely end.

German anti-aircraft artillery, efficient from the start of the war, had become increasingly deadly and to it the peril of enemy fighters would soon be added. When air fighting began in earnest it was quite common for young pilots just out of Britain, with very limited training, to last no more than ten weeks. In earlier and less hectic times, Corbett Wilson had survived for ten months. He did not live to experience 'The Fokker Scourge' during late 1915 and early 1916 when the supremacy of the German fighters caused huge RFC casualties nor a later repetition that marked 'Bloody April' in 1917 before the Allies finally regained their power in the air. In CW's pre-war pioneering days he could not have begun to envisage the aeroplane as a deadly weapon at the heart of Armageddon. Had he survived the war his passion for mechanical matters and aviation might have contributed to developments in peacetime flying. But this could also be said of many of the gallant airmen whose future was cruelly cut short.

Denys Corbett Wilson and Isaac Newton Woodiwiss lie side-by-side in well-tended graves in the British Cemetery at Cabaret-Rouge, Souchez.

CHAPTER TWENTY-THREE

Envoi

The sad news of the death of her devoted son was communicated officially to Mrs. Corbett Wilson at her Knightsbridge apartment where many letters of condolence were received. Amongst them was a letter from CW's Commanding Officer.

Dear Mrs Corbett-Wilson:

You will have heard by now of the sad death of your son. He was killed by a shell whilst doing a reconnaissance over Fournes. A German aviator dropped a message yesterday to say that he and his observer, Woodiwiss, were both killed instantly and were being buried at a cemetery at Fournes.

   When I advance I will try to locate the spot and mark it.

   I can't say how sorry I am to have lost your son. He was as gallant a fellow as I know, and he is much missed by us all. His kit has been sent to Cox & Co., Charing Cross, and an inventory by post.

Allow me to offer you my sincerest sympathy,
Yours sincerely,
D. S. LEWIS
(Major).

From Major General Trenchard, GOC 1st Wing RFC, and a staunch supporter of CW's ideas:

Dear Mrs Wilson,

I am very sorry to have to write and tell you that your son, Corbett Wilson, is missing. He left on May 10th with an officer called Woodiwiss for a reconnaissance on a Parasol Morane, and has not returned, and on May 11th the Germans dropped a message from one of their aeroplanes to say that artillery had hit one of our machines and that the two officers were killed and were being buried in the cemetery East of Fournes in German lines.

I fear this machine was the one your son was in, as it was about the correct time, and they called the machine a parasol aircraft.

I must say that we all feel his loss terribly, even in this terrible war. He was one of the most gallant officers I have met, and one of the best. He did not know what fear was; he always did his work splendidly. He was very popular with all, and would have made a name for himself.

If I ever get the chance I will try and find the place at Fournes and will try and come and see you after the war.

Yours sincerely

Hugh M. Trenchard
1st Wing,
Royal Flying Corps
British Expeditionary Force

———————————

From a comrade:

> Cheveny,
> Hunton,
> Maidstone.

Dear Mrs Corbett Wilson

I cannot tell you how terribly sorry I was to read of Denys' death, or how much I sympathise. As you know I was in the same squadron with him in France, and so can realise what his loss must mean to you and also to the RFC. He was always so cheerful and so absolutely regardless of personal danger that he was an inspiration to everyone else. I can only join with everyone else who knew him in expressing my deepest sorrow and sympathy.

Yours very sincerely,
A. D. BORTON.

Please do not trouble to answer this.

CHAPTER TWENTY-FOUR

Remembrance

In Ireland, Denys Corbett Wilson and his exploits are not
forgotten. At the spot in Crane where his record flight ended,
a suitably inscribed bronze memorial records the event. Not
far away, outside Wexford County Museum in Enniscorthy, a
similar plaque stands. Inside, there are several mementoes. In a
hotel across the way from the museum, a conference suite called
the 'Corbett Wilson Room' features a series of photographs of
the man and his machine.

For the past thirty years Kilkenny Aerodrome, which is
located not far from Darver House, has held an annual 'Fly-in
and Air Show' dedicated to the local hero. A suitably inscribed
solid silver model of CW's Bleriot is the principal award. Thus
his peacetime exploits are marked in the country that was his
temporary home.

In France, in September 2004, the British Air Services
Memorial was dedicated at St Omer. In his address of welcome,
Air Marshal Sir Frederick Sowrey (who contributed the
Foreword to this book) greeted the guests:

It is only right that the memorial should be at St Omer, the
main supply base for aircraft and equipment of every sort
and the site of the Royal Flying Corps' Headquarters. Many
squadrons were formed on this airfield and operated over
the trenches and beyond. A tangible and poignant
reminder of what this involved is to be found in the

'Souvenir' Cemetery, just quarter of a mile from where we stand today, where nearly 150 members of the British Air Services are buried – the largest single group of those who fell on the Western Front – drawn from every part of the Commonwealth.

In passing, the Air Marshal mentioned that his own father, together with two brothers, all members of the RFC, had operated in the area. The splendid memorial is further enhanced by metal pillars that depict the number and crest of all units, including No. 3 Squadron in which CW so nobly served. Though relatively unknown, amid the great names of 'the war to end wars', Denys Corbett Wilson is not forgotten.

Index

NOTE: The names of places frequently flown over by Denys Corbett Wilson, and the occurrence of the title Toyal Flying Corps (R.F.C.), together with the words Bleriot and Moranes, are purposefully give only initial mentions in this Index.

1st Corps, 71, 149
Aircraft Park, the 28
Allied artillery 159, 68, 90, 136, 148
Alsace 39
American 128
Amiens 26
Alne 97
anti-aircraft artillery 48
'Archibalds' 122
Archies 139
Ardaloo 19
Argonne 107
Armentiers 75, 77
armoured train (German) 115, 120
Ashford 40, 52
Aviatik German aircraft 126
Avro 504 29, 113, 118
Battle of the Marne 30
Belgian resistance 37
Bengal Cavalry 57
Berlin 66, 84, 86, 88, 98

Bethune 74, 82, 83, 94
Black Watch, The 123
Bleriot 83, 84, 85 . . .
Bleriot serial no. 1872 151
Bleriot XI 7, 8, 83, 84, 85, 90 . . .
Bleriot, Louis 6
'Bloody April' 152
Boulogne 26, 34, 128
Bristol 26
British Air Services Memorial 156
British Expeditionary Force (B.E.F.) 29, 30
British War Cemetery 152
Brooklands 16
Brussels 41
Bryant, Loftus 25, 26, 140
BÚC 21, 56, 57
Byrne, Elizabeth 2

Cadogan Gardens 53
Calais 22, 59
Camberley 45
Cameron Highlanders 119
Castiglione 34
Central Flying School 22
Chantilly 129
Chester 11
Choques 62
Christmas journals 66
Clonmel 19, 21
Coldstream Guards 98

173

Collin, Ferdinand (L. Bleriot's manager) 5
Colva 12
Corbett Wilson, Corbett-Wilson, family 1
'Corbett Wilson Room' 156
Courtrai 96
Curtiss Aircraft Company 17

Daily Mail 68, 85, 92
Damer, Leslie Allen 10
Darver House 2, 26
Davis, Miss Trehawke 26
Dieppe 22
Dijon 25, 34
Dixmunde 73
Don 149
Donnehan 138
Doolittle, Gen. J. (U.S.) 88
Dorset Regiment 2
Douglas, W. Sholto (later Lord Douglas of Kirtleside) 102
Dover 28
Dover Patrol, The 47
Dowding, Hugh (later Lord Dowding) 45
Dublin 79
Dunkerque 76

Egypt 58
English Channel 53
Enniscorthy 18
Essen 86, 98, 99, 107
Estaires 74
Eton College 2, 65

Farnborough 22, 24, 32, 35, 37, 39, 51, 126, 140
Fertahert 100
Fethard 15, 17
Field Magazine 106
First Corps 71, 149
Fishguard 12, 13, 22
Five Years in the R.F.C. 138

Fournes 153, 154
French Aero Club 5
French Air Force 9
French army exercises 22
French Territorials 142
French, John, Gen. Commanding B.E.F. 49, 111

Garros, Roland 39, 40
Genoa 44, 45
Givenchy 93, 96, 97
Gnome rotary engine 78
Goodwick 12
Gorey 24

Hans Crescent 69
Harrods 142, 147
Henderson, David, Brig, Gen. 22
Hendon Aerodrome 4, 10, 26
Henri Farman Aircraft 70
Heslis 96
Hewitt, Vivian 16
Highlanders 34, 118
Hinges 73
Holyhead 11, 79
Hotel du Palais, Paris 34
Howitzer Granny 59, 148

Illustrated Newspapers 81
Imber Court 2
Indian troops 58, 66, 67, 68, 84, 87, 149
Irish Aviation Museum 19
Irish Sea 79
Isle of Wight 26
Italy 124

'Jock' (CW's dog) 42, 61, 73, 97 . . .
Jodphur Lancers 66
Joffre, Gen. (overall Allied commander) 111
Jura Mountains 3

Kaiser Wilhelm II 33

Kilkenny 2, 18, 43, 61, 156
Kilkenny air display 156
Kilkenny city 18, 156
King George V 22
King's Royal Rifles 107
Kitchener's New Army 51

La Bassee 77, 87, 91, 93 . . .
Langres 25
Lausanne 25
Le Bourget Airport 127
Le Cateau 29
Le Havre 28
Le Rhone (aircraft engine) 129,
    131
Liege 35, 39
London Scottish 118
Loraine, Robert 76, 77, 79, 80, 82,
    83, 88

Manchester Regiment 98
Maubeuge 28
Merville 106
Messines 73
Mons (the retreat from) 29, 135
Moranes 101, 106
Mulhausen 106
Munster Fusiliers 29

Namur 42
Naples 44, 45
Nassau 17
Netheravon 22
Neuve Chapelle 97, 98, 100, 135,
    138, 141, 151
newspapers 12, 14
Ninth Lancers 49
No.2 (Aeroplane) Coy. 24
No.3 Squadron 22, 28, 30, 71 . . .
N.3 Squadron R.F.C. 22, 28, 30,
    71 . . .
Nos. 1 and 2 Wings 31

Pau 4, 6, 38

Pearl Harbor 88
Penguin, The 5
Peyton, Gen. 36
Phoenix Park 17, 79
Pietro 26, 27, 106, 144
Potet (mechanic) 25, 26
Powerstown Racecourse 19
Punch magazine 66
Puncherstown Races 15

Queen's Bays Cavalry Regiment
    36
Queen's County 2
Quinn, I Mrs. H 18

R.F.C. aircraft 29
Reims International Display 8
Rhine 94, 106
Rhyll 17
Roberts, Lord 71, 75
Royal Aero Club 10
Royal Aircraft Establishment 51
Royal Flying Corps, foundation
    of 22
Royal naval Volunteer Reserve 17

Salmond, Maj. Gen. J. 141
Salome 120
Sandhurst 151
Scots Guards 43, 98, 145
Seguin Brothers 8
Selmet, M. 6
Shaw, George Bernard 79
Sketch newspaper 117
Soissons 119
Sopwith Aircraft 43
South African War 2
Southampton 37
Sowrey, Sir Freddy 156
Spahis (French cavalry) 146
St. Omer, R.F.C. Field
    Headquarters 54, 63, 72, 82,
    83, 106, 156
St. Pol 130

Sussex 22
Sussex Regiment 147
Sykes, Col. Frederick 84

Taube, German aircraft 58
Territorials 37, 142
The Aeroplane magazine 19
The Bays Cavalry Regiment 59
'The Fokker Scourge' 152
Third Division 31
Titanic 14
Transvaal 2
Trenchard, Major Gen. Hugh 2,
    76, 88, 89, 98, 100, 113, 123,
    126, 141, 142, 154

Union Flag 24
Union Jack 53

Vickers Gun Bus aircraft 78
Villa D'Este (Lake Como) 26
Voisin Aircraft 76

Warvin 77
Waterford 22, 26
Waterloo 34, 114
Welles 26
Western Front 32
Woodiwiss, Lt, Isaac Newton 151
Wright Brothers 8, 79

Zeppelins 39